Party Images in the American Electorate

Party affiliation has long been the driving force behind electoral politics in the United States. Despite this fact, scant attention has been devoted to the American electorate's party images—the "mental pictures" that individuals have about the parties which enable citizens to translate events in the larger political environment into terms meaningful to them as individuals. Party images are central to understanding individuals' political perceptions and, ultimately, voting behavior.

Party Images in the American Electorate systematically examines the substance, evolution, and manipulation of party images within the American public over the last half century, both within the public as a whole and within important subgroups based on class, race and ethnicity, sex, and religiosity. Ultimately, this important book investigates how these party images are tied into the story of party polarization and how they affect electoral outcomes in the United States.

Mark D. Brewer is Assistant Professor of Political Science at the University of Maine. He is the author of *Relevant No More? The Catholic/ Protestant Divide in American Electoral Politics*; and co-author of *Diverging Parties*; *Split: Class and Cultural Divides in American Politics*; and *Parties and Elections in America*, 5th edition.

Party Images in the American Electorate

Mark D. Brewer

Routledge
Taylor & Francis Group

NEW YORK AND LONDON

First published 2009
by Routledge
270 Madison Ave, New York, NY 10016

Simultaneously published in the UK
by Routledge
2 Park Square, Milton Park, Abingdon, Oxon OX14 4RN

Routledge is an imprint of the Taylor & Francis Group,
an informa business

© 2009 Taylor & Francis

Typeset in Goudy by
RefineCatch Limited, Bungay, Suffolk
Printed and bound in the United States of America on acid-free
paper by Edwards Brothers, Inc.

Library of Congress Cataloging-in-Publication Data
  Brewer, Mark D., 1971–
  Party images in the American electorate / Mark D. Brewer.
    p. cm.
  Includes bibliographical references and index.
  1. Political parties—United States—Public opinion.
2. Democratic Party (U.S.)—Public opinion.   3. Republican Party
(U.S.: 1854–)—Public opinion.   4. Public opinion—United States.
5. United States—Politics and government.   I. Title.
  JK2271.B74 2008
  324.273—dc22   2008027775

ISBN10: 0–415–96275–7 (hbk)
ISBN10: 0–415–96276–5 (pbk)
ISBN10: 0–203–88449–3 (ebk)

ISBN13: 978–0–415–96275–9 (hbk)
ISBN13: 978–0–415–96276–6 (pbk)
ISBN13: 978–0–203–88449–2 (ebk)

For my parents

Contents

List of Figures and Tables

Figures

Tables

Preface

To borrow a phrase from Walter Lippmann, this book is about "the pictures in our heads."[1] More specifically, this book is about the pictures of their political parties that Americans have in their heads. In other words, the focus here is on the images that Americans hold of the Democratic and Republican Parties.

Given how important parties and partisanship are to understanding American politics, party images in the American electorate have been grossly under-examined by scholars. We devote incredible amounts of attention and energy to uncovering the essential elements of party identification, the vagaries of vote choice, the dynamics of partisan change, and the list could go on and on. All of this attention and energy is justified—these are important matters, critical to making sense of politics in the United States. But I argue that party images are just as critical. We need to know what comes into Americans' minds when they are asked to think about and evaluate the Republicans and the Democrats. Partisan evaluations by citizens are in many ways fundamental to the political process in the United States. The American system virtually demands that citizens evaluate the words and actions of political parties and their representatives, and then act on the basis of those evaluations. Since we know that human beings are "cognitive misers"—they use stereotypes and other mental shortcuts to process information and make decisions—the mental pictures that Americans have of their political parties are likely to be central to understanding individual political behavior.[2] This book shows how Americans see the Democratic and Republican Parties. There are no overly complicated analyses. All I am interested in is fleshing out what images pop into Americans' heads when they think about the two major parties in the United States. The chapters that follow present and discuss these images.

This book was a relatively long time in coming to fruition as it was regularly put on hold so that other projects could be completed, and thus I have a long list of people to thank. I will begin with my fellow members of the University of Maine community. My colleagues in the Department of Political Science are a truly exceptional group of people, and the environment they create is highly conducive to research and writing. I also need to thank my students in a number of courses over the past few years. We regularly discussed many of the ideas found in this book, and their insights were quite helpful as I worked my way through this project. A Summer Faculty Research Award from the Office of the Vice President of Research was enormously helpful in the early stages of this project, and discussions with colleagues in the Politics and Society Group sharpened the final product.

The staff at Routledge played an important role in bringing this project to completion. My editor, Michael Kerns, was highly supportive of the project, and is a joy to work with. This is our second project together, and I look forward to many more. Michael's assistant, Felisa Salvago-Keyes, was always quick to respond to my questions, and her keen attention to detail made the process run very smoothly. Liz McElwain did an outstanding job of copyediting the manuscript in a short period of time.

My biggest debt of gratitude is owed to my family. My wife, Tammy, was as always incredibly supportive during this process, and never complained about the extra time at the desk that I had to put in to get this book finished, even though more often than not she needed to be putting in extra desk time as well. In most cases the extra time spent working on this project also came at the expense of my wonderful children, Megan and Jack. Now that this is completed there will be more time for stories and ballgames of all different types. Finally, I thank my parents, to whom this book is dedicated. I would not be where I am today without them. I close with the standard caveat—I am solely responsible for any and all errors contained herein.

Chapter 1

Pictures of Parties

In a now famous line, E.E. Schattschneider once said that democratic governance in the United States would be "unthinkable" without political parties.[1] And despite many changes in American politics, most knowledgeable observers of American elections would still agree with Schattschneider. No other social characteristic or issue position even comes close to party identification in affecting individual vote choice. No other heuristic or information shortcut is used more often by voters as they decide for whom to cast their ballot. Simply put, partisanship has long been and continues to be the driving force behind the outcomes of American elections.[2]

Given the importance of partisanship for American elections, surprisingly little scholarly attention has been devoted to how the two main political parties are viewed by the electorate in terms of substance. In other words, little empirical research has been done on the *party images* held by the American electorate. Do Americans tend to see the parties in economic terms, or foreign policy terms, or in terms of cultural issues? We simply do not know. The major work in this area is now over thirty years old,[3] and more recent pieces focused on the substantive component of these party images have been few and far between.[4] This book presents the images Americans hold of the Republican and Democratic Parties and discusses what significance these images have in American electoral politics.

WHY PARTY IMAGES MATTER

This relative dearth of attention is an important matter. Party images, simply put, are the "mental pictures" that individuals have about the parties. They are people's evaluations of what the parties stand for and who they represent. For example, many Americans see the Democratic Party as the party of the working class in the United States, while a common image of the Republicans involves the GOP as the party supportive of limited government. While these party images are generally very broad, and quite often somewhat simplistic or confused, they do represent what comes into individuals' minds when they think about the parties and are central to understanding individuals' political perceptions and ultimately political actions.[5] Party images are an essential comprehension mechanism, enabling citizens to translate events in the larger political environment into terms that are meaningful to them as individuals.[6] Party images provide the necessary link between the elite level and mass level in American politics.[7] Because they are easy to form and to remember, party images provide a very useful and efficient framework for individuals to utilize in their interpretation of political candidates, events, and information in general.[8] It may not be too much of an exaggeration to claim, as Charles Sellers does, that party images are the major determinants of the political alignment at the mass level.[9]

Over the years political scientists have devoted an enormous amount of energy and attention to determining the factors that influence partisanship and vote choice, justifiably so given the importance of these phenomena. In the 1940s and early 1950s, Paul Lazarsfeld and some of his colleagues at Columbia University conducted a series of studies that led them to conclude that social group memberships were the primary determinant of individuals' electoral behavior. In the famous words from *The People's Choice*: "[A] person thinks, politically, as he is, socially. Social characteristics determine political preference."[10] While not entirely dismissing the importance of social group identities, Angus Campbell and his colleagues at the University of Michigan argued in *The American Voter* that psychological factors were far more important in shaping an individual's electoral behavior. A person's psychological attachment, or affect, toward a political party was especially important here—identification with a specific party, determined to a high degree for many Americans by the partisanship of their parents, was the driving force in vote choice.[11] Following up on the work of Campbell et al., Norman Nie and his colleagues painted a different picture of individuals' electoral behavior. According to their findings in *The Changing American Voter*, individuals made electoral decisions largely based on their evaluations of candidates and issue positions.[12] Finally, Morris Fiorina—building on the work of V.O. Key, Jr.—argued that what really drove electoral behavior was voters' retrospective evaluations of how political parties and their officials had performed in office. If voters determined that an office holder had performed well, the politician and her or his party were rewarded by voters. If the evaluation was negative, voters turned to the opposition party.[13]

The debate over what determines electoral behavior rages on, far from anything even remotely resembling closure. The reality is that each of the four explanations briefly outlined above has merit, and rises and falls in relevance depending on the individual voter and on the circumstances of a particular election. But, for our purposes, what is really important is the connection between the proposed dynamics of electoral behavior and party images. If group membership is seen as crucial to vote choice, then party images rooted in which groups the parties represent will play an important role. If psychological affect toward the parties is what matters, then certainly the ways in which an individual sees a particular party matter a great deal. If issues drive partisanship and vote choice, then how a person sees a party on the issue(s) of importance will be key in determining how he or she acts on Election Day. Finally, if retrospective evaluations are the deciding factor, voters will have to use the party images they hold at least in part to make the proper connections between elected officials, parties, and performance in particular areas. In short, no matter which explanation of electoral behavior one prefers, party images matter.

The importance of party images to American electoral politics is by itself more than enough to merit their further investigation. There are, however, a number of additional reasons to take a closer look at the images Americans have of their political parties. As noted above, there has been little empirical work on this subject over the years, and even the little that has been done is now somewhat dated.[14] Much has changed in American politics in recent years, and it is certainly possible that these developments have affected the party images held by the American electorate.

This first change that comes to mind is the dramatic increase in the importance of partisanship among political elites (especially members of Congress) since the 1970s. In addition to becoming more internally cohesive in their voting behavior, the parties at the elite level have also become more ideologically polarized from each other.[15] These increases in cohesion and polarization are not the result of pointless partisan bickering; they are, in fact, driven by increasingly large divisions between the Republican and Democratic Parties in government over the proper direction of public policy and course of American society.[16] In other words, the increasing importance of partisanship among elites is rooted in substance. As Daryl Levinson and Richard Pildes phrased it, "the two major parties today are as coherent and polarized as they have been in perhaps a century."[17]

A second, but clearly related, change pointing to the need to investigate party images is the growing importance of partisanship in the general public. After declining throughout the 1960s and 1970s, partisanship at the mass level has rebounded significantly in recent years. Fewer citizens now vote for candidates from more than one political party, the percentage of citizens who identify themselves as "strong" partisans is up, and the effects of partisanship on individual vote choice are either at or approaching the levels last seen in the 1950s, the supposed golden age of parties.[18]

It is likely that the growing significance of partisanship to the average voter is due at least in part to the growing partisan divisions at the elite level. As Sharon Jarvis explains it, when the elite voices speak in partisan terms, partisan labels take on greater meaning for the masses.[19] Increased partisan conflict among elites primes members of the general public to rely more on partisan cues and judgments in shaping their own political participation.[20] It is necessary, however, to caution against placing sole responsibility for the resurgence in mass partisanship in such an elite-driven, top-down process. After all, why would partisan elites (at least those elites elected to office) change their behaviors in the first place unless there was some pressure on them from the mass public to do so?[21] Regardless of the cause,[22] greater importance of partisanship among the general public certainly has implications for the party images held by that same public.

A third reason to scrutinize the public's party images is the increasing sophistication of the American electorate. Research indicates that issue awareness has expanded among Americans, and also that positions on issues have become more relevant to individual vote choice.[23] In addition, American voters have become much more ideological in recent years, and the impact of conservative and liberal ideology on vote choice has increased dramatically over the past few election cycles.[24] Such developments must hold some significance for Americans' party images.

Fourth, and perhaps most important, partisan conflict has expanded into new issue areas over the last thirty years. In addition to the traditional New Deal era partisan conflict over issues of economic equality, the parties now differ on racial and cultural issue areas as well. Partisanship increasingly affects views on these types of issue among both elites and the mass electorate.[25] It only makes sense that as partisan conflict spreads to new battlefields, the images of the parties held by the general public could change in response.

It is easy to see how any or all of the developments described in the above paragraphs could have easily altered the party images present in the American electorate. Americans might "see" the political parties much differently today than they did twenty-five, fifteen, or even ten years ago. Of course, it is also the case that changes in party images could have significantly contributed to these same developments. When these possibilities are combined with the important role that party images play in American electoral politics and the lack of an empirical investigation of what these party images are, it is evident that a thorough examination of the subject is called for. This book provides such an examination.

THE PLAN OF THIS BOOK

As stated earlier, party images are the mental pictures that individuals have of specific political parties, in this case the Democratic Party and the Republican Party. These images are the thoughts and visuals that pop up in a person's head when she or he is asked about, or otherwise is given cause to think about, either the Republicans or the Democrats. There are theoretically a number of different ways in which one could go about determining the substance of Americans' party images, but the option utilized in this book involves examining what Americans say they like and dislike respectively about the Democratic and Republican Parties. While much more will be said on this decision in the next chapter, it needs to be stated here that these likes and dislikes are a particularly useful tool to investigate and flesh out the mental pictures Americans have of their two major parties. Likes and dislikes are incredibly easy for individuals to form and also to remember.[26] To provide a useful comparison, how many people have difficulty remembering what they like and dislike about certain foods, or what they like and dislike about certain television programs? Partisan likes and dislikes can and do function in much the same fashion. More than that, a good deal of content can be encapsulated within a simple like or dislike. When an individual holds a particular like or dislike for a specific party, he or she is giving voice to a belief about what the party stands (or does not stand) for, and who the party supports (or opposes). These are obviously crucial pieces of information.

Determining what Americans like and dislike about the Republicans and the Democrats should allow us to dramatically increase our understanding of electoral politics. To summarize Samuel Popkin's view of the American electorate in a ridiculously short sentence, voters know things.[27] And one of the most important things that they know is what they like and dislike about their political parties. Voters are informed on the issues and groups they care about, and they are especially informed on where the parties stand on these issues and groups.[28] Partisanship is an incredibly powerful and effective cue that citizens use when making political decisions, including the decisions they make in the voting booth.[29] The stereotypes that individuals have of the parties are a crucial component of this idea of partisanship as cue.[30] The likes and dislikes Americans have of their parties enable us to get at these stereotypes.

This book digs into these partisan likes and dislikes. The goals here are simple, but important. First, I present the substance of Americans' party images. The question of what comes into Americans' minds when they think about the Republicans and the Democrats is answered. Second, I examine how these images have changed over time. The stability and evolution of party images tell us a great deal about how American politics has unfolded over the past half century. Finally, in the last chapter I discuss the importance of party images in contemporary American politics.

The book begins with an examination of party images as they exist within the American electorate as a whole. From there, we move to examinations of party images as they exist on both sides of four crucial, ongoing cleavages within the American electorate—class, race, sex, and religious salience. Each of these divisions is treated in a separate chapter. Finally, conclusions about the significance of party images are reached. But before we get there, we need to see what specifically Americans like and dislike about their parties. Chapter 2 addresses this matter.

Chapter 2

Party Images in the Electorate as a Whole

As noted in the previous chapter, likes and dislikes are simple yet important judgmental heuristics. Individuals almost automatically assess what they like and what they dislike about a particular person, object, or situation that they encounter, and then use these likes and dislikes as guides for additional assessments in the future, and ultimately as guides to action if and when action is called for. A good deal of substantive information can be compacted into a simple like or dislike, effectively summarizing the information and cataloging it for future use. We all know what we like and what we dislike and why we like and dislike these things, and these judgments matter when we contemplate just about everything we encounter in our daily lives. For example, this morning I made breakfast for my wife and two children. The menu comprised bacon, scrambled eggs, hash browns, toast, and bananas. I like bacon, hash browns, and toast, and so I readily placed some of each on my plate. I do not like eggs or bananas, and thus I did not take either of these foods. Likes and dislikes—about anything—are important.

It follows then that Americans' likes and dislikes of their two major political parties also matter. To a certain degree, Americans evaluate the Democrats and the Republicans in the same way I sized up my breakfast options: they determine what they like and what they dislike, and then they act accordingly. Admittedly, determining what one likes and dislikes about political parties is a bit more complicated than giving thumbs up or down to breakfast foods. Parties are not monolithic, and one is highly unlikely to have as much information on the GOP as she or he possesses on wheat toast. But, still, typical Americans know a good deal about the Democrats and Republicans, whether they realize it or not. Politics is conducted and discussed in overwhelmingly partisan terms in the United States, and one would be hard pressed to find political commentary without partisan cues and references. Even those who try to avoid politics altogether are highly unlikely to be successful in such an attempt. In the course of their day-to-day activities they will encounter information about politics and government, and a good deal of that information will contain partisan references.[1]

Americans should be relatively well positioned to hold at least some basic likes and dislikes of the Republican and Democratic Parties. This book—following in the tradition of the relatively few substantive works on this matter—uses these likes and dislikes to determine the images that Americans have of their two major political parties.[2] These images are the mental pictures that come into a person's mind when she or he thinks about either the Democrats or the Republicans. For example, a commonly held image of the Democratic Party is that of the party as the champion of the common person, while a widely held image of the Republicans involved the party as the defender of conservative principles. As Richard Trilling puts it, "The likes and dislikes Americans have for their parties, that is, their party images, can be interpreted to demonstrate the perceived meaning of these parties."[3]

Unlike many phenomena that are of interest to the empirical researcher, party images are relatively easily examined. The American National Election Studies (ANES) has, since 1952, consistently (in presidential election years) asked its respondents if there is anything that they like and then if there is anything that they dislike about both the Democratic and the Republican Parties. The questions are open-ended, and respondents are allowed to offer up to five answers to each query.[4] While some have raised concerns that the open-ended nature of party likes/dislikes questions may introduce bias based on education level or articulation skills,[5] such fears seem unwarranted.[6] As John Geer points out, open-ended questions represent the types of questions that respondents are likely to deal with in everyday life. It is the closed-ended questions more commonly found in survey instruments that represent an unfamiliar setting for those answering the questions.[7] In addition, a strong case can be made that any disadvantages to the open-ended nature of the likes/dislikes questions are far outweighed by the fact that the data these questions generate are not shaped by predetermined response categories and provide a remarkably consistent measure over time.[8] All data utilized in this study come from *The ANES 1948–2004 Cumulative Data File* (see Appendix).[9]

AMERICANS' PARTY IMAGES—HOW PREVALENT?

What do we know about Americans' images of their two major political parties? Beginning with some basic contours, we know that partisan likes and dislikes tend to be relatively common within the American electorate, and that these likes and dislikes have become even more prevalent over the last twenty to thirty years. Figure 2.1 presents the percentage of

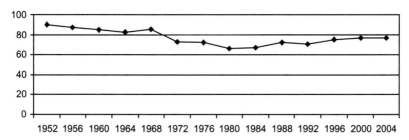

Figure 2.1 Percentage of respondents with at least one partisan like or dislike, 1952–2004.

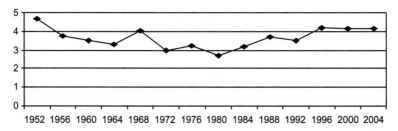

Figure 2.2 Mean party salience (sum of all Democratic and Republican likes and dislikes), 1952–2004.

Americans able to express at least one like or dislike of the Republican or Democratic Parties from 1952 to 2004. After consistently being in the 80 to 90 percent range throughout the 1950s and 1960s, the percentage of Americans with at least one partisan like or dislike began to decline in the early 1970s, and reached a low point of 66 percent in 1980. From that point, the number of Americans having at least one like or dislike of their parties has slowly gone back up, reaching 77 percent in both 2000 and 2004. Throughout the time period under consideration here, a substantial majority of Americans have at least one thing that they like or dislike about their political parties.

Another way of gauging how prevalent party images are among Americans is to measure the average number of partisan likes and dislikes held by individuals. This information is presented in Figure 2.2. Here we see that the average American has more than one partisan like or dislike; in fact, the average has been a bit over four in each of the last three presidential election years. The averages for these three years are higher than that of any other year in the time series with the exception of 1952, and represent a sizeable increase from the low point of 2.71 likes/dislikes in 1980. The results presented in Figure 2.2 give us confidence that Americans do indeed have things that they like and dislike about the Democrats and the Republicans. It also merits pointing out that, not surprisingly, the average number of partisan likes and dislikes that a person holds increases as education increases, as Figure 2.3 demonstrates.[10] But, even here, Americans at all education levels have things that they like and dislike about the parties.[11]

What happens when we separate out these responses by likes and dislikes and by party? Figure 2.4, which presents the mean number of likes and dislikes by party, sheds some initial light on this question. A number of interesting points present themselves in this figure. The first thing one notices is that the Democratic Party is generally the subject of a higher number of likes and dislikes than is the Republican Party.[12] Only twice—in 1972 and 1992—did the GOP garner a higher number of likes or dislikes than the Democrats, and even in these years the end result was a virtual tie. One also notes that over time the Democratic Party tends to be evaluated more positively than its Republican counterpart, although the GOP has increased its average number of likes since 1980 (with the exception of 1992). We will return to this point momentarily. One final point to note in figure 2.4 is that, since 1980, likes and dislikes for both parties have increased significantly. This means that Americans are finding more to like and dislike about their parties.

Finally, Figures 2.5 and 2.6 allow us to compare the parties in terms of average total likes and dislikes on the part of Americans. Figure 2.5 presents

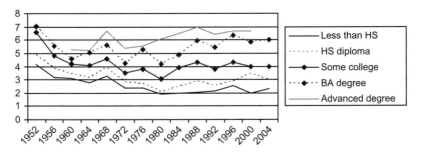

Figure 2.3 Mean party salience by education level, 1952–2004.

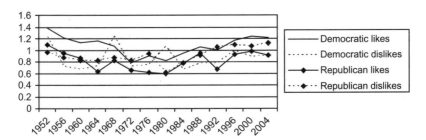

Figure 2.4 Mean number of likes and dislikes of the Democratic and Republican Parties, 1952–2004.

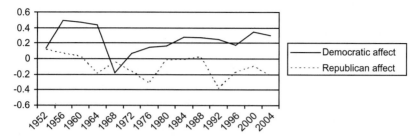

Figure 2.5 Mean Democratic and Republican party affect (likes minus dislikes), 1952–2004.

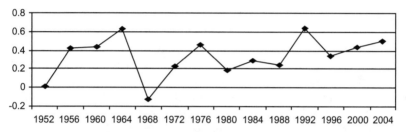

Figure 2.6 Mean net party affect (Democratic likes and Republican dislikes minus Democratic dislikes and Republican likes), 1952–2004.

the *affect* (likes minus dislikes) for each party, while Figure 2.6 presents the net *party affect* (the sum of Democratic likes and Republican dislikes minus the sum of Democratic dislikes and Republican likes). Figure 2.5 indicates that, with the exception of 1968, the Democrats have always had a more positive affect than the Republicans, often by a substantial margin. Indeed, 1968 represents the only year in which the Democrats had a negative affect, while the GOP has had a positive affect only once since 1960, and only four times overall since 1952. Figure 2.6 reinforces the greater warmth toward the Democrats as opposed to the Republicans. In this figure, a positive number represents a Democratic advantage while a negative number indicates an edge to the Republicans. Only in 1968 does the line dip into negative territory. In most years, the Democrats have a significant edge in net party affect.

THE SUBSTANCE OF PARTY IMAGES

So we know that party images are relatively widespread within the electorate, that they have been increasing since the early 1980s, and that more often than not the Democratic Party is seen in a more favorable light than is the Republican Party. But what about the substance behind these images? What, specifically, do Americans tend to like and dislike about their two major political parties?

Fortunately, the ANES allows us to address these questions. As noted earlier, the partisan likes/dislikes questions are open-ended, and respondents are allowed to offer up to five responses (likes or dislikes) to each query. Only the respondents' *first offerings* are utilized here. While a case could certainly be made for using all responses, I am more interested in getting at the images that are most salient to respondents, represented by those likes and dislikes that come to mind first when individuals are asked for their normative take on the Democrats and the Republicans. Thus, for this study, each respondent could potentially offer as many as four combined likes/dislikes or as few as zero in a particular year.[13]

The ANES records the open-ended responses, and I use these responses to create seven substantive categories, with "no mentions"—when respondents failed to offer a like or a dislike—accounting for an eighth category.[14] Economic images contain likes and/or dislikes related to specific economic policies such as tax cuts or unemployment compensation, as well as references to economic groups such as the working people, the poor, or business. Non-economic domestic images are made up of references to domestic policy areas that are not directly economic in nature. Examples here include likes and dislikes related to civil rights, abortion, or capital punishment. Party philosophy images comprise ideological references (e.g., liberal or conservative), statements about broad values the party stands for or against, and likes and dislikes related to the parties' views on government. Government management images have to do with the nuts and bolts of governing in the form of references to efficiency, or corruption. General party images are made up of references such as "I just like [or dislike] the party" or "I was born a Democratic and I'll die one too." Images related to people in the party are made up of references to particular individuals within the party, or to a lesser extent general references about the quality or lack thereof of the officials or leaders in the party. Finally, foreign policy images are made up of references to dealings with other nations and all war and military references.

Keeping these eight categories in mind, what comes into Americans' minds when they are asked what they like and dislike about their political parties? Table 2.1 represents a first cut at this question, combining the first-mention likes and dislikes for both the Democrats and Republicans, and presenting them by substantive category.

A number of points worth noting emerge from Table 2.1. First, the number of no mentions rises in the 1970s and 1980s before declining beginning in the 1990s. This matches with the information presented in Figures 2.1 to 2.3 that Americans have become increasingly likely to have images of the parties in recent years. Turning to the substantive categories, economic images of the parties have been quite stable in magnitude over

Table 2.1 Subject area of all possible party first mentions, 1952–2004

Year	No mention	Economic	Non-economic domestic	Party philosophy	Government management	General party image	People in the party	Foreign policy
1952	46	22	4	6	4	8	5	4
1956	51	16	5	4	2	9	9	4
1960	55	15	4	8	1	10	3	5
1964	54	12	4	9	2	11	5	2
1968	51	11	3	9	2	13	6	4
1972	59	14	2	7	2	8	5	3
1976	60	15	2	9	3	6	3	1
1980	62	14	2	8	3	7	3	2
1984	60	13	3	10	2	6	3	3
1988	55	16	4	9	3	6	2	4
1992	56	15	5	11	3	6	2	2
1996	52	14	7	13	3	7	2	1
2000	52	14	8	13	3	7	2	1
2004	51	13	7	16	3	8	2	3

Note: Percentages sum across, and may not sum to 100 because of rounding. See endnote 14 for information about the make-up of the categorization scheme utilized here.

Source: American National Election Studies, respective years. First mentions only.

the period under examination here, and until the 1990s were clearly the dominant component of party images. Since that time, however, images having to do with party philosophy have significantly increased, and philosophical images now rival (and in 2004, exceed) economic images. Images of the parties grounded in non-economic domestic issues were stable and relatively uncommon from the 1950s to the 1980s, but have gained ground since the 1990s. General images of the parties have remained stable with the exception of a spike in the 1960s, and appear relatively frequently. Images having to do with people in the parties were more common in the 1950s and 1960s than they have been since, despite the supposed development since that time of candidate-centered politics. Finally, for both parties considered together, images having to do with government management and foreign policy have consistently been few in number over the entire period.

What do images look like when the parties are examined individually? Table 2.2 addresses this matter for the Democratic Party. A first look here reveals that, despite some small decline from the figures seen in the 1950s and early 1960s, economic images continue to be the most common images of the Democratic Party, and also that this category is much more positive than negative for the party. Mirroring the trend noted for the overall images presented in Table 2.1, non-economic domestic images of the Democrats have increased since the 1990s, and the party is seen in net positive terms here as well. Images having to do with the Democrats' philosophy, relatively prevalent throughout the entire period, have increased significantly since the mid-1980s. Here the party is viewed more negatively than positively, usually by a small margin. General party images of the Democrats have been relatively stable with the exception of the 1960s, and usually tend to be slightly more negative than positive. Pictures of the Democrats having to do with people in the party have consistently been few in number and generally evenly matched in terms of positives and negatives, while images of the Democrats rooted in government management and foreign policy tend to be relatively uncommon (with the exceptions of 1952 and 1968)[15] but negative for the party.

Table 2.3 presents the same information for the Republican Party. Here, too, economic images have tended to dominate, especially in the period before the 1990s, but the economic images of the GOP held by the public are much more negative than positive. As was the case for the Democrats, non-economic domestic images of the Republican Party have risen since the 1990s, but unlike the Democrats these images tend to be slightly more negative than positive for the Republicans. Philosophical images have increased for the Republicans as well. This is to the party's benefit as its philosophical images tend to be much more positive than negative, the opposite of the Democrats' situation. This has consistently been the case since 1952. The percentage of government management images tends to

Table 2.2 Positive and negative images of the Democratic Party by subject area, 1952–2004

Year	No mention Pos.	No mention Neg.	Economic Pos.	Economic Neg.	Non-economic domestic Pos.	Non-economic domestic Neg.	Party philosophy Pos.	Party philosophy Neg.	Government management Pos.	Government management Neg.	General party image Pos.	General party image Neg.	People in the party Pos.	People in the party Neg.	Foreign policy Pos.	Foreign policy Neg.
1952	37	45	38	10	8	3	6	10	—	11	7	8	4	5	—	9
1956	44	58	32	3	7	4	3	5	0	2	9	12	6	9	0	7
1960	43	64	29	3	4	4	6	10	—	1	14	10	2	2	—	5
1964	41	60	26	4	6	6	5	12	2	4	15	9	4	3	2	3
1968	49	44	22	4	6	5	5	11	2	4	12	17	5	6	—	10
1972	57	59	22	6	3	1	5	10	—	2	7	10	2	8	2	3
1976	55	63	28	6	2	2	5	13	—	4	5	6	3	3	0	4
1980	54	64	22	9	4	2	9	9	—	4	7	7	2	3	—	3
1984	55	64	19	7	4	2	12	12	—	2	7	6	2	3	—	3
1988	51	59	25	9	5	3	11	13	—	4	6	7	2	2	—	3
1992	52	59	23	8	10	3	11	13	—	6	5	7	2	2	0	1
1996	49	54	21	8	10	5	11	17	2	5	6	8	2	1	0	2
2000	44	57	23	6	10	6	13	15	—	3	5	9	2	3	0	2
2004	47	54	20	5	8	5	14	16	—	4	7	11	2	3	—	2

Note: Percentages sum across, and may not sum to 100 because of rounding. See endnote 14 for information about the make-up of the categorization scheme utilized here.

Source: American National Election Studies, respective years. First mentions only.

Table 2.3 Positive and negative images of the Republican Party by subject area, 1952–2004

Year	No image Pos.	No image Neg.	Economic Pos.	Economic Neg.	Non-economic domestic Pos.	Non-economic domestic Neg.	Party philosophy Pos.	Party philosophy Neg.	Government management Pos.	Government management Neg.	General party image Pos.	General party image Neg.	People in the party Pos.	People in the party Neg.	Foreign policy Pos.	Foreign policy Neg.
1952	52	50	12	28	2	3	6	4	5	—	10	7	8	4	5	2
1956	50	53	7	23	3	7	5	2	4	—	7	6	17	6	8	2
1960	54	57	7	20	2	5	10	4	2	—	10	5	6	2	8	5
1964	64	52	4	15	2	3	13	5	1	2	8	14	5	8	2	1
1968	57	55	3	14	2	3	13	6	2	—	12	13	6	6	5	—
1972	65	56	4	23	2	2	8	4	2	3	7	7	6	3	6	3
1976	69	54	5	21	—	2	12	6	3	2	5	9	3	4	3	2
1980	67	63	7	17	—	3	9	5	4	—	6	7	3	2	3	—
1984	62	61	7	17	2	4	11	7	3	2	7	3	4	2	5	4
1988	56	56	13	19	3	4	9	5	4	4	6	5	3	2	7	5
1992	65	49	7	24	4	6	9	8	3	4	5	6	2	2	5	2
1996	57	49	7	19	5	8	16	10	6	3	6	9	1	2	2	0
2000	56	50	9	18	7	8	16	10	4	3	5	8	2	2	2	—
2004	55	47	8	18	5	7	14	10	3	4	8	9	2	1	5	3

Note: Percentages sum across, and may not sum to 100 because of rounding. See endnote 14 for information about the make-up of the categorization scheme utilized here.

Source: American National Election Studies, respective years. First mentions only.

be relatively small for the GOP, but the Republicans do tend to be seen as better managers than the Democrats. General party images have been quite stable and, for the most part, closely balanced for the Republicans. Images having to do with people in the party have declined for the GOP (see 1956—it appears everyone really did like Ike), although the relative balance within this image category has remained in place. Finally, foreign policy images are more common (although still quite low in number) for the Republicans than they were for the Democrats, and they also tend to be more positive.

This chapter addresses one last matter in terms of the substance of Americans' party images. Specifically, I want to deal with specifics. What particular like or dislike is the most common for each party? Table 2.4 presents this information. The economic advantage of the Democrats is readily apparent. For every year, the top like of the Democrats was that they were the party of the working class and the common person, while the top dislike of the Republicans was that they were the party of big business and the upper class. Both of these were the top choices by wide margins, especially the dislike of the GOP because of their perceived support of the wealthy and big business. The percentage of respondents with these images has also been remarkably stable over time. The Republican edge based on images having to do with party philosophy is also visible in Table 2.4. Since 1964 the top like of the GOP has been its perceived conservatism, while with the exceptions of 1952 and 1956, the top Democratic dislike has been some variation of the party's liberalism, particularly its liberalism having to do with the size and spending of the federal government. Ideological images have become more prevalent over time. The electorate tends to view the Democrats positively on social class concerns, but sees the GOP in a more positive light when it comes to party philosophy. This Democratic edge on economic issues is long-standing, while the Republican advantage rooted in party philosophy has increased over the duration of the time period examined here.

CONCLUSION

What have we learned from this examination of party images as they exist within the electorate as a whole? First, we can clearly see that Americans have a good deal that they like and dislike about the Republicans and the Democrats, and that these likes and dislikes have increased since the early 1980s.[16] We also see that for the vast majority of the time the Democratic Party is viewed more favorably overall than is the Republican Party. In terms of substance, we see that economic issues still dominate the images Americans have of their parties, and that the traditional New Deal division between the parties remains in place.[17] The economic image tends to

Table 2.4 Top image for Democratic and Republican likes and dislikes, 1952–2004

Year	Democratic like	Democratic dislike	Republican like	Republican dislike
1952	Party of working class	Corruption/graft/dishonest	Time for change	Party of big business and upper class
1956	Party of working class	Negative campaign	Dwight Eisenhower	Party of big business and upper class
1960	Party of working class	Too much government spending	Republicans peace party	Party of big business and upper class
1964	Party of working class	Too much government spending	Conservatism	Party of big business and upper class
1968	Party of working class	Too much government spending	Conservatism	Party of big business and upper class
1972	Party of working class	George McGovern	Conservatism	Party of big business and upper class
1976	Party of working class	Too much government spending	Conservatism	Party of big business and upper class
1980	Party of working class	Welfare/poverty policies	Conservatism	Party of big business and upper class
1984	Party of working class	Too liberal	Conservatism	Party of big business and upper class
1988	Party of working class	Too liberal	Conservatism	Party of big business and upper class
1992	Party of working class	Too much government spending	Conservatism	Party of big business and upper class
1996	Party of working class	In favor of big government	Conservatism	Party of big business and upper class
2000	Party of working class	In favor of big government	Conservatism	Party of big business and upper class
2004	Party of working class	Too liberal	Conservatism	Party of big business and upper class

advantage the Democrats. At the same time that economic images have remained prevalent, images rooted in party philosophy have grown significantly in recent years. The growing salience of ideology is a crucial component of this rise, and has worked to advantage the Republicans, although a fair number of Americans view the Democrats positively because of party philosophy as well. This is important given the increasing impact of ideology on party identification and vote choice that was discussed in the previous chapter. Non-economic domestic images have also risen (although not nearly as much as party philosophy images), and here the Democrats have a slight edge. Finally, the GOP tends to get a small but steady advantage from foreign policy images, and to a lesser extent from government management images as well.

These are the images within the electorate as a whole. But what happens when we start dicing it up? Chapter 3 will begin to answer this question when we start dicing on the basis of class.

Chapter 3

Party Images and the Class Cleavage

THE PLACE OF CLASS IN AMERICAN POLITICS

Social class. The concept has generated a fair amount of attention over the years among those interested in American government and politics. Some, such as Alexis de Tocqueville, have argued that the United States is largely a classless society, and that as such class-related concerns are usually not terribly prevalent in American politics.[1] Others, such as V.O. Key, are skeptical of such claims and therefore assign a much greater importance to class in American political life. As Key put it, "Politics generally comes down, over the long run, to a conflict between those who have and those who have less."[2]

Leaving aside the question of whether or not Tocqueville was correct when he wrote *Democracy in America* (first published in 1835), American history contains a number of eras where class conflict was clearly at the center of the nation's political dialogue. The heyday of the Populists in the late 1880s to mid-1890s is certainly one such period, and at least some would claim that the Progressive Era of the early twentieth century is another.[3] If there is a single era in American politics where almost everyone can agree that social class was front and center, it is the New Deal. One would be hard pressed to find a scholar of this period who does not believe that the politics of the New Deal era—at least until the onset of World War II—were all about class conflict.[4]

We saw the results of this New Deal class conflict in the overall party images presented in the previous chapter. In every presidential election year since 1952, the most common reason individuals give for liking the Democratic Party is that the Democrats are the party that looks out for the working class and the common person in American society, while the most common (by a huge margin every year) dislike of the Republican Party is that the GOP is dedicated to serving the interests of big business and the more affluent. If one believes that politics during the New Deal was a classic example of Key's battle between the haves and the have-nots—and most do—it is clear that the residue from that conflict has remained important in the years that followed, even up to the present day. When the average American thinks about the divisions between the Republicans and the Democrats, she or he is more likely to envision a cleavage rooted in social class than any other division.

There is little doubt that class drove American politics during the New Deal era, or that class-related themes remain important for the images Americans hold of the Democratic and Republican Parties. There has, however, been a good deal of disagreement about the importance of class in recent political conflict. The biracial lower class coalition that Franklin Roosevelt crafted for the Democratic Party during the New Deal was always somewhat unstable simply because of the toxicity of race relations in the United States. FDR was able to hold the coalition together, but after his death in 1945 its viability was much more open to question. Indeed, in hindsight some have seen the ultimate demise of the New Deal coalition actually being determined as early as the years 1946–1948.[5] By the late 1960s, Republican strategist Kevin Phillips prophesied that the era of class politics would soon be over (if it wasn't already), and that Democratic Party dominance would end with it.[6]

By the late 1980s and early 1990s many researchers were making the case that Phillips' prediction had come to pass: the New Deal coalition was dead, and class politics were a thing of the past.[7] For some, race was the factor that ultimately rendered social class unimportant in American politics.[8] For others, it was racial issues combined with resentment over high taxes.[9] Still others attributed the declining relevance of class to a combination of racial and especially social issues, such as abortion and gay rights.[10] Finally, a number of analysts, the most prominent of whom is Ronald Inglehart, laid the declining importance of class at the feet of the emerging post-industrial society. In this relatively affluent post-industrial society, the majority of people no longer had to be concerned with issues of immediate material needs, and therefore turned their attention to non-material quality-of-life issues. This reduced the importance of social class and opened the door for other cleavages to rise in importance.[11] Nicol Rae argued that the declining importance of class in American politics was in many ways a return to normalcy. Only in extraordinary conditions—such as the Great Depression—did class dominate American politics. In normal times, cultural issues (which Rae defined to include social and racial issues) were more important in shaping political conflict and defining the political agenda.[12]

At just about the same time that many were writing the obituary for class politics in America, a funny thing happened. Class—at least as measured by income levels—began increasing in importance for individuals' electoral behavior. Less affluent Americans increased their support of the Democratic Party, while better-off Americans did the same for the Republican Party.[13] Even the South, long insulated from class politics by the stifling issue of race, began to show signs of class meaning-fully affecting individuals' party identification and vote choice.[14] In his 1972 evaluation of class and American politics, Richard Hamilton reported finding little impact of class, primarily because there was a clear majority in favor of liberal social welfare policies and because so many members of the middle and upper middle class were Democrats. Class simply did not mean much in terms of electoral behavior.[15] Thirty years later, things had clearly changed. For partisanship and vote choice, class mattered.

There are a number of reasons why class matters politically in con-temporary America. The first, and perhaps most important, is the high degree of economic inequality present in the United States. In terms of both income and wealth, the United States has much higher levels of inequality than just about all other developed nations.[16] Moreover, after declining from the end of World War II through the early 1970s, inequality has been on the rise ever since.[17] In recent years, the degree of inequality has reached levels not seen since the Roaring Twenties or per-haps even the Gilded Age. When levels of inequality are high in a society, the members of that society tend to notice. And if the society is a free one, chances are good that the inequality in question will become an issue in the public debate.

Whether or not the debate amounts to anything in terms of electoral divisions, however, depends on the degree to which the political parties differ on issues related to class. In the U.S., this division has long existed between the parties. Throughout their respective histories, the Democrats and the Republicans have clearly differed on issues related to social class and inequality. The Democrats have traditionally been far more con-cerned with economic inequality, and thus have tended to present them-selves as the party of the less fortunate in American society and as the party more willing to use the power of the state to produce greater equal-ity. In contrast, the Republican Party has long been the champion of individualism in economic life. The GOP tends to be far more supportive of the interests of business and the more affluent, and is wary of—if not outright hostile to—the use of the government power to affect individual economic outcomes.[18] The stands of the parties on class issues were clear during the New Deal, and if anything have perhaps become more clear since the 1980s and the two presidential terms of Ronald Reagan.[19] Despite the claims of some, the parties differ on class issues, and these differences are readily apparent to the American electorate.[20] As William Mayer described it, on economic issues "liberals and conservatives in America have been fighting much the same battle, from the same picket lines, for most of this [twentieth] century."[21] Those picket lines are also party lines.

PARTY IMAGES AND CLASS DIVISIONS

Clearly there are reasons why we might expect class divisions to be relevant in the images that Americans have of their political parties. Even though Trilling reported declining class differences in party images in 1976, it is possible that this situation has reversed. As discussed above and demonstrated in Figure 3.1, class divisions in electoral behavior have been growing in American society. Figure 3.1 presents the differences between thirds of the income distribution on presidential vote, but the pattern is also the same for House of Representatives vote and party identification. Since 1972, those Americans in the lower third of the income distribution have tended to be more supportive of the Democratic Party than have those in the middle third, and to an even larger extent, those in the upper third.

This is the picture we would expect to see if class differences matter politically. It must be noted that class is measured here using family income levels.[22] Certainly other options to measure class are available, and no doubt some may object to the use of income. Self-identified class is an option that is sometimes used to measure class, as is occupation. A few researchers also use education as a proxy for class. None of these indicators is perfect, and in an ideal world I would prefer to use an indicator made up of all of the above components in addition to a measure that tapped into wealth. However, in the real empirical world such an indicator is not available, at least not in the ANES. I ultimately choose family income as the best measure of class available because, in a debate involving questions of the opportunities available to individuals and the resources on hand to take advantage of those opportunities, income is the more important factor.[23]

When we look at party images by income level, what do we see? Figure 3.2 presents a first cut at this question, with mean party salience (all likes and dislikes combined) by income third. Here we see that those in the upper third of the income distribution have a higher number of likes

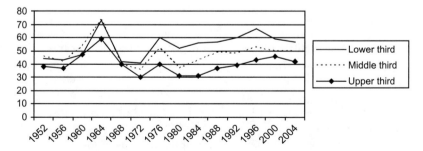

Figure 3.1 Democratic presidential vote by income third, 1952–2004.

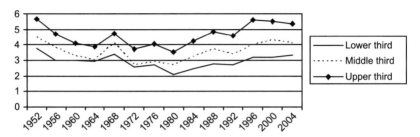

Figure 3.2 Mean party salience (sum of all Democratic and Republican likes and dislikes) by income third, 1952–2004.

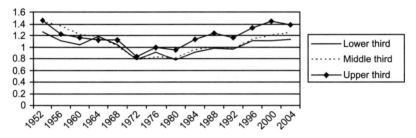

Figure 3.3 Mean number of likes of the Democratic Party by income third, 1952–2004.

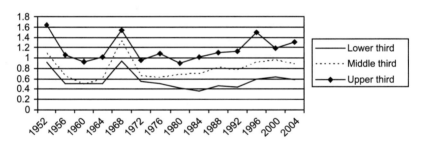

Figure 3.4 Mean number of dislikes of the Democratic Party by income third, 1952–2004.

and dislikes of the parties than do those in the middle third, or the lower third. This likely reflects the correlation of income with education, and the fact that those with higher levels of education are more likely to have partisan likes and dislikes of the parties. Figure 3.2 also shows that the magnitude of party images bottomed out for all three income groups in 1980, before rebounding to levels that in 2004 closely approached the 1952 high points for the time series.

What happens when we separate out responses by likes and dislikes and by party? Figures 3.3 to 3.6 provide the answers to this question. Looking

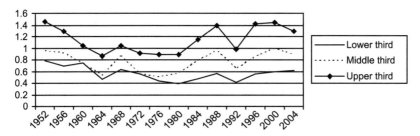

Figure 3.5 Mean number of likes of the Republican Party by income third, 1952–2004.

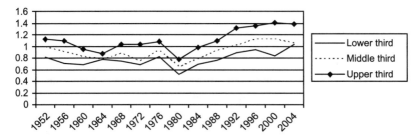

Figure 3.6 Mean number of dislikes of the Republican Party by income third, 1952–2004.

first at likes of the Democratic Party (Figure 3.3), we see that the number of positive images of the Democrats has risen since 1980 for all three income groups, and also that those in the upper third tend to have a higher average number of likes. However, the gap in mentions between those in the upper and lower thirds is not nearly as large as it was for the total salience figures presented in Figure 3.2. As for Democratic dislikes (Figure 3.4), it is clear that those in the middle third and especially those in the upper third of the income distribution tend to have a much higher number of negative images of the Democrats than do those in the bottom third. These figures for the Democratic Party provide some qualified support for differentiation of party images on the basis of social class. The average number of Democratic dislikes rises as income rises, and while those in the upper third also tend toward a higher average number of likes of the Democrats, the distance between the income groups is quite small.

What about the images of the Republican Party? As Figure 3.5 presents, those in the upper income third tend to have a much higher average number of Republican likes than do those in the middle or lower third. We also see that although likes of the GOP have risen among all three income groups since the mid-1970s, the increase has been most pronounced among those in the top third. This clearly lends support to a class effect in the expected direction on party images. Figure 3.6, on the other hand, demonstrates a possible class impact on party images, but in the opposite direction than one would expect. Dislikes of the Republican Party have become more common among all income groups since 1980, but throughout the time period they have been the most prevalent on the part of those in the upper income third. Again, the correlation of income with education and the fact that higher education produces more likes and dislikes is likely to be at play here, but still, a situation where those in the upper third of the income distribution see the GOP more negatively than do those in the lower third does not support a polarization of party images by class, at least not in the manner we would expect.

Figure 3.7 combines the likes and dislikes for each of the parties into a net party affect measure. Positive numbers represent a net pro-Democratic edge in image, while negative numbers represent a Republican advantage. Here we can clearly see a much more pronounced Democratic advantage among the less affluent. Even here, however, it must be noted that while those in the upper third are not as pro-Democratic as those in the lower third, they are also not overwhelmingly pro-Republican. In most years, those in the upper third are closer to neutral (0) than anything else. So, again, we have some qualified support for a division of party images by class.

What happens when we turn to the substance behind these likes and dislikes? Beginning first with the Democratic Party, Table 3.1 presents subject areas of the Democratic likes by income third, and Table 3.2 does the same for Democratic dislikes. Looking at the likes, two things jump out immediately. First, there is no significant difference between the income groups in terms of having *something* that they like about the Democrats, and, second, there is also no clear pattern of difference between the groups in terms of liking the Democratic Party for economic reasons. Economics is the top category for all three income groups, which does not support a difference in party images by class. Other findings worth noting from Table 3.1 are the rise in non-economic domestic reasons for liking the party among those in the upper third since the

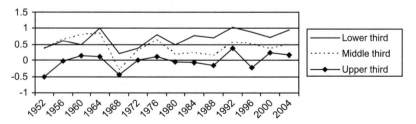

Figure 3.7 Mean net party affect (Democratic likes and Republican dislikes minus Democratic dislikes and Republican likes) by income third, 1952–2004.

Table 3.1 Subject area of likes of the Democratic Party by income third, 1952–2004

Year	No mention			Economic			Non-economic domestic			Party philosophy			Government management			General party image			People in the party			Foreign policy		
	L	M	U	L	M	U	L	M	U	L	M	U	L	M	U	L	M	U	L	M	U	L	M	U
1952	44	35	37	31	43	41	6	7	5	5	6	6	0	1	1	8	5	6	4	3	3	1	1	2
1956	48	40	45	30	35	31	7	5	4	2	3	5	0	0	0	8	9	9	5	6	5	0	1	1
1960	50	42	46	27	33	28	5	4	4	2	5	7	1	0	1	12	13	11	2	2	2	1	1	2
1964	41	41	45	24	27	27	7	6	5	3	3	4	2	3	2	18	13	12	3	6	3	2	1	2
1968	50	52	47	19	23	22	6	4	6	3	4	8	2	1	1	15	11	10	5	5	5	1	0	1
1972	57	58	55	21	24	23	5	2	4	5	5	7	1	0	0	8	8	6	2	2	3	2	1	2
1976	53	56	51	28	29	30	2	2	3	3	4	8	2	1	1	8	5	4	3	3	2	0	0	1
1980	54	55	49	20	22	25	4	4	5	6	9	13	2	1	1	11	5	4	3	2	3	1	1	0
1984	56	55	49	20	19	19	4	3	4	8	12	17	1	0	1	7	7	6	2	2	3	0	1	1
1988	54	52	44	23	24	26	4	3	6	8	11	16	1	1	1	8	6	5	2	2	1	0	1	2
1992	51	53	48	26	21	23	4	6	7	8	12	15	2	1	1	6	5	4	2	2	2	1	0	0
1996	47	52	42	27	18	20	6	11	14	6	12	16	2	1	1	10	4	5	2	2	2	2	0	0
2000	47	47	36	22	22	25	8	8	17	11	13	17	2	3	3	7	5	3	2	2	2	2	0	0
2004	51	47	46	20	23	18	4	7	10	11	12	14	1	1	1	9	8	6	3	1	2	2	1	2

Table 3.2 Subject area of dislikes of the Democratic Party by income third, 1952–2004

Year	No mention			Economic			Non-economic domestic			Party philosophy			Government management			General party image			People in the party			Foreign policy		
	L	M	U	L	M	U	L	M	U	L	M	U	L	M	U	L	M	U	L	M	U	L	M	U
1952	59	50	34	8	10	11	3	4	3	7	8	14	7	9	15	4	4	7	4	4	6	8	11	9
1956	69	62	42	3	4	5	2	4	3	2	4	8	1	2	3	9	11	17	7	9	11	7	5	9
1960	68	73	54	3	4	5	4	3	3	5	6	17	0	0	1	10	8	12	2	2	3	6	5	4
1964	72	65	49	2	4	3	5	6	4	7	8	17	3	4	6	6	7	11	1	2	4	3	4	4
1968	55	47	38	4	3	6	4	5	4	5	10	15	3	3	5	15	15	17	5	6	7	10	11	9
1972	68	64	46	3	5	11	1	—	2	5	10	14	2	1	1	11	7	13	5	9	9	4	2	3
1976	76	65	48	3	4	11	1	1	2	6	11	21	2	4	5	5	8	6	3	3	3	4	4	3
1980	75	62	53	5	10	12	—	2	2	5	9	14	3	4	6	6	8	9	3	3	3	3	3	2
1984	77	64	47	4	6	11	3	2	3	6	12	21	2	1	2	5	7	8	2	4	4	3	3	4
1988	73	57	45	3	9	14	2	3	3	6	13	19	2	4	7	8	7	7	1	3	3	3	4	3
1992	74	59	43	4	6	14	3	3	4	7	14	19	4	5	8	7	8	7	2	2	4	—	2	1
1996	70	57	34	6	5	13	3	5	8	8	17	25	3	5	6	8	7	11	0	1	2	2	—	2
2000	69	55	42	3	6	9	5	6	8	10	15	21	3	5	4	7	8	11	1	4	4	1	2	1
2004	68	53	37	3	3	7	4	6	5	10	17	24	4	5	4	9	11	13	1	2	5	2	3	3

1990s, and the rise in a positive image of the party based on party philosophy among all income groups, but most among the top third, since 1980. Again, neither of these supports a class structuring to party images.

We see greater support for such a structuring in Table 3.2. Here we see that those Americans in the upper third are far more likely to have a dislike of the Democratic Party than are those in the middle or lower thirds, and also that the dislike is more likely to be based on economics among the upper third. The largest differences between the income groups, however, come from the party philosophy category. Those in the upper third have long had a more negative image of the Democratic Party based on party philosophy than those in the lower or middle third, and this division has grown over time. In the Democratic dislikes, we do see support for a class effect on party images.

Tables 3.3 and 3.4 present the likes and dislikes respectively of the Republican Party by income thirds. Beginning first with the likes (Table 3.3), we see that those in the upper income third are more likely to have something that they like about the GOP and also more likely to see the party positively for economic reasons, both of which support a class structuring of party images. Those in the upper third are also more likely to see the GOP favorably for reasons grounded in party philosophy, which could also support a class division. It should also be noted that the percentage of positive party philosophy images of the Republicans has risen among all income groups over time, and also that the GOP is more likely to be seen positively due to foreign policy than is the Democratic Party. As for the negative images of the Republicans (Table 3.4), we do not see much to support a class structuring here. Those in the upper income third are more likely to have a dislike of the GOP and the percentage of respondents within each income group viewing the Republicans in a negative fashion for economic reasons is quite high, neither of which supports a view of party images shaped by class. We also see in Table 3.4 that the percentage of Americans viewing the GOP negatively for non-economic domestic reasons and party philosophy reasons has increased across the board, but has increased most among the upper third of the income distribution.

Readers might recall that in Chapter 2 I presented the top specific like and dislike for each party by year. This information is not presented in this chapter simply because it tells us very little that has not been noted already. The top reason for liking the Democratic Party for every year and each income group was that the party looked out for the working class with one exception, and that exception was that the top Democratic like of those in the lower third in 1984 was that the party represented the interests of the poor and needy. The same universality applies for disliking the GOP because it is the party of big business and the upper class (with two exceptions here—the lower third's top dislike of the GOP in

Table 3.3 Subject area of likes of the Republican Party by income third, 1952–2004

Year	No mention			Economic			Non-economic domestic			Party philosophy			Government management			General party image			People in the party			Foreign policy		
	L	M	U	L	M	U	L	M	U	L	M	U	L	M	U	L	M	U	L	M	U	L	M	U
1952	62	56	42	7	7	5	2	2	3	8	7	14	3	4	6	8	8	13	5	10	11	4	7	5
1956	60	52	36	5	6	8	2	3	3	3	4	9	4	4	8	6	6	7	12	17	21	9	8	6
1960	61	62	51	5	6	7	2	2	2	3	6	16	3	2	2	12	7	8	6	6	6	8	9	8
1964	72	72	56	3	2	4	2	2	2	5	9	21	1	1	2	8	6	7	5	5	5	3	3	2
1968	65	57	48	3	3	3	1	2	4	6	13	21	3	3	2	11	13	10	5	6	6	5	4	5
1972	69	69	55	4	3	6	2	2	3	4	9	10	2	3	3	8	6	8	6	3	9	6	5	6
1976	77	73	57	3	4	8	1	2	2	6	9	18	2	2	5	5	4	4	3	2	2	2	3	3
1980	76	67	53	4	7	12	1	1	2	7	10	12	1	4	8	4	6	7	3	3	3	2	3	4
1984	75	61	47	3	8	13	2	3	1	4	10	18	2	3	3	8	6	6	3	5	6	4	4	6
1988	70	54	41	6	13	19	2	3	4	5	9	13	3	4	4	5	5	7	4	3	2	4	9	10
1992	77	67	51	3	5	12	3	6	5	4	8	15	3	3	3	5	4	6	2	2	3	5	5	5
1996	71	57	39	3	8	11	2	6	9	10	17	21	5	5	8	6	5	7	—	1	2	2	2	3
2000	70	54	40	4	9	14	6	7	9	8	17	23	3	4	6	6	4	4	—	3	2	1	3	2
2004	64	56	43	4	8	13	4	5	5	11	13	17	3	2	4	8	9	8	2	2	2	5	5	7

Table 3.4 Subject area of dislikes of the Republican Party by income third, 1952–2004

Year	No mention			Economic			Non-economic domestic			Party philosophy			Government management			General party image			People in the party			Foreign policy		
	L	M	U	L	M	U	L	M	U	L	M	U	L	M	U	L	M	U	L	M	U	L	M	U
1952	59	50	47	28	30	27	2	3	4	3	0	4	0	0	0	6	6	9	1	5	6	1	2	3
1956	61	53	46	20	25	23	7	7	7	1	1	4	0	1	2	6	6	7	4	6	8	1	2	4
1960	63	58	47	17	21	19	6	7	6	1	4	7	1	1	1	8	6	8	2	2	3	2	2	8
1964	55	56	49	17	16	13	3	3	3	3	2	6	2	2	2	14	11	15	5	8	11	3	2	1
1968	63	56	46	13	15	15	4	2	2	3	7	10	1	1	2	11	11	15	4	7	10	1	1	1
1972	62	59	47	20	23	25	2	2	2	3	3	6	2	3	3	6	6	8	3	2	4	2	2	4
1976	58	54	48	20	21	24	1	2	2	4	7	8	3	2	2	8	10	10	4	3	4	1	1	2
1980	68	62	57	17	18	19	1	3	4	3	6	7	2	1	1	6	7	7	2	2	3	1	—	2
1984	61	61	53	16	16	19	5	5	5	6	6	11	2	2	3	4	4	4	2	2	1	5	5	4
1988	63	56	48	15	21	23	3	5	6	4	4	7	3	4	5	6	5	3	2	2	2	5	5	5
1992	55	51	40	27	22	23	3	5	9	3	9	13	3	5	4	6	5	6	2	1	2	2	2	2
1996	55	49	39	18	21	20	6	9	9	6	10	14	2	3	3	8	8	10	2	1	4	1	0	0
2000	59	49	37	19	20	19	5	8	13	6	10	15	2	4	4	7	7	9	1	2	2	1	1	0
2004	51	50	36	21	17	16	5	8	11	6	9	15	3	5	4	9	7	13	2	0	1	3	4	4

1952 was because it was the party of the "Hoover depression" and the most common Republican dislike of the upper third in 1964 was Barry Goldwater). And for all income thirds, the top Republican like, at least since 1968, has almost always been the party's conservative ideology or something closely related to it. Only among Democratic dislikes do we see anything even remotely resembling variation. Here the middle and upper thirds are quite consistent in disliking the Democrats for something related to the party's liberal ideology (again, post-1968), while those in the lower third have a more variable list of top dislikes. But even here, in six of the ten presidential election years from 1968 to the present, the most prevalent dislike of the Democratic Party has been related to the liberalism exhibited by the party.[24]

CONCLUSION

So where does this leave us? Certainly there are some clear class differences in party images of Americans. Americans in the lower third of the income distribution have a significantly higher net affect (favorable) for the Democratic Party than do those in the top third. Those in the lower third are also much more likely to see nothing likeable about the Republican Party. Those in the upper income third, on the other hand, are much more likely to dislike the Democratic Party, in particular for economic and especially party philosophy reasons. Those in the upper third also exhibit much more positive images of the GOP, especially for party philosophy and economic reasons.

But it is important not to push the class difference case too far here. Those in the upper third are more likely to have images of the parties across the board, likely as a result of higher levels of education. Yes, the more affluent see more to like about the GOP, but they also see more to like about the Democrats as well, in addition to more to dislike about both parties. Perhaps even more important, roughly equal percentages of those in all three income groups like the Democratic Party for economic reasons, and dislike the Republicans on the same basis. So the bottom line is somewhat mixed here. There are undoubtedly some class differences in party images, but they are not as pronounced as one might expect given the high levels of inequality present in the United States and the clear differences between the Democrats and Republicans on class issues. In terms of party images, class does indeed matter but not as much as it theoretically could.

Chapter 4

Party Images and Race and Ethnicity

In his classic treatise on the subject, Gunnar Myrdal famously called the issue of race in the United States "an American Dilemma." In the introduction to his 1944 work, Myrdal wrote:

> The American Negro problem is a problem in the heart of the American. It is there that the interracial tension has its focus. It is there that the decisive struggle goes on . . . The "American Dilemma," referred to in the title of this book, is the ever-raging conflict between, on the one hand, the valuations preserved on the general plane which we shall call the "American Creed," where the American thinks, talks, and acts under the influence of high national and Christian precepts, and, on the other hand, the valuations on specific planes of individual and group living, where personal and local interests; economic, social, and sexual jealousies; considerations of community prestige and conformity; group prejudice against particular persons or types of people; and all sorts of miscellaneous wants, impulses, and habits dominate his outlook.[1]

Despite his somewhat tortured language, Myrdal captured a good deal of the tension that has surrounded, and continues to surround, the issue of race in America. It is the tension that exists between the worship of a national ideal celebrating the belief that all human beings are created equal and a two-hundred-plus-year reality where American society has routinely failed to meet this national ideal. While such inequality has existed on a number of fronts, on no front has the inequity been as heinous as that having to do with race. Unequal treatment is at the heart of discussions over race in the United States. In the famous words of Martin Luther King, Jr., "All we say to America is, 'Be true to what you said on paper.' "[2] On issues relating to race, the United States has far too often failed to meet King's request.

HOW RACE AND ETHNICITY MATTER

Most would agree that the United States has come a long way on the issue of race and ethnicity, and in a relatively short period of time. No one would confuse the America of 2008 with the America of 1963. Equal treatment under the law despite differences in race and/or ethnicity is now firmly in place and overwhelmingly supported by the American public, and this same public is now much more tolerant and accepting of racial and ethnic differences and interaction between the races in a wide variety of areas. However, despite such improvements, very few knowledgeable observers of American politics would be willing to assert that we have reached a point where race no longer matters in American politics. Indeed, the last thirty years have seen the rise of a substantial subfield within the American political science community where the primary activity involves somewhat heated disputes over exactly why and how race matters for contemporary American politics.

Perhaps the most prevalent argument for the manner in which race plays out in current American politics is usually referred to as "symbolic" racism, or less often as "new" racism. Originally explicated by David Sears and Donald Kinder, and exponentially expanded on over the years by both men together and separately with a seemingly endless number of coauthors, symbolic racism holds that the old-style Jim Crow racism—outright hatred on the basis of race and support for unequal treatment on the basis of race—is largely a thing of the past. Today's racism—symbolic racism—is rooted in a combination of negative feelings toward blacks (and other racial and ethnic minorities as well) and beliefs that minorities fail to adhere to some of America's most fundamental values—in particular, individualism and self-responsibility.[3] This symbolic racism leads whites to resent African Americans and other racial and ethnic minorities in certain instances, especially in situations where whites perceive that minority groups receive undeserved benefits or special treatment from government. In a more recent piece, Kinder (with coauthor Lynn Sanders) labeled this new form of prejudice "racial resentment," and according to some it has a powerful impact on current politics in the United States.[4]

Some scholars, perhaps most vocally Paul Sniderman and Thomas Piazza, argue that the symbolic racism view is simply wrong. For Sniderman and Piazza, it is not that race no longer matters, but that it matters in a way that is different from the symbolic racism school. Here race is relevant in the form of the old-fashioned racism outlined above, at least in some cases. Sniderman and Piazza also argue that not all white opposition to policies designed to benefit racial and ethnic minorities is rooted in racism, a point echoed by a number of others.[5]

Still others who have contemplated the manner in which race still matters in American politics have reached different conclusions from those outlined above. Lawrence Bobo argues that, for the vast majority of whites in American society, the commitment to racial and ethnic equality is real. However, their support for policies designed to produce such equality is far more limited, primarily because of self-interest. Some whites see blacks and other minorities as competing with them for scarce resources and beneficial outcomes, and thus oppose policies that put them at what they perceive as a disadvantage. Here a form of group conflict explains why race and ethnicity still matter.[6] For others, most notably Mary Jackman, a white desire to remain dominant over racial and ethnic minorities is the reason for the continued relevance of race.[7]

In spite of a situation that Charlotte Steeh states "appears to be a morass of contradictory findings," the one thing on which all of the scholars cited above (and many others) agree is that race continues to be very important in American politics.[8] There is much evidence to support such a view. Research consistently shows that blacks and whites differ significantly in their opinions on a wide variety of issues. These differences are largest, not surprisingly, on racial policy issues, but exist across the spectrum of issues on the public agenda.[9] Among African Americans, the inequality that continues to exist on the basis of race and ethnicity is seen primarily as a result of prejudice on the part of whites; whites, on the other hand, are much more likely to see minorities as responsible for the inequalities that exist, in many instances, they may feel, because minorities are lazy and refuse to work hard enough to get ahead.[10] Certain issue areas in particular, such as welfare and crime, are especially affected by racial attitudes and stereotypes.[11] Certainly many of the phenomena discussed in this paragraph have been in place the longest in the dynamic between whites and blacks in the United States, but certainly many of the same differences can be seen as existing between whites and Latinos in the U.S. as well.

As was discussed in the previous chapter, differences between groups in the electorate are one thing. These differences becoming important politically are another. For group differences to become relevant politically, the parties must recognize these differences and react to them. More than that, the parties must give voice to the differences in question; the Republicans and the Democrats must disseminate divergent messages, take divergent stands, and present divergent policies related to the differences in question in order for those differences to matter politically. When dealing with group differences on the basis of race and ethnicity, we do not need to ponder this matter for too long. The Democrats and the Republicans clearly differ on issues related to race and ethnicity, and these differences are now longstanding.

The Democratic Party began its move in a liberal direction on questions of race during the New Deal era. While Franklin Roosevelt was undoubtedly very careful to avoid antagonizing southern Democrats on the issue

of race—and certainly some powerful voices in his administration regularly pushed him to do more, most notably his wife Eleanor and Secretary
of the Interior, Harold Ickes—the New Deal president did reach out to
blacks and successfully brought many of them into the ranks of the
Democratic Party. Harry Truman accelerated this leftward movement
of the Democrats on race when, in the years 1946 to 1948, he created a
presidential commission on civil rights, became the first president to
ever address the NAACP, and desegregated the American military by
executive order. The 1948 Democratic Party Platform also contained a
very liberal (for its time) plank on civil rights, further establishing the
party as liberal on race.[12] However, it was not until 1964 that the differences between the parties on issues of race became entirely clear. In 1964,
the Democrats—at least those outside of the South—had successfully
pushed through the Civil Rights Act of that year and were promising
to do even more to address racial inequality as they campaigned for the
November elections. On the other hand, the Republicans—even though
many GOP lawmakers had also helped to secure passage of the Civil
Rights Act—nominated Arizona Senator Barry Goldwater for the presidency. Goldwater was one of only a handful of non-southern senators to
vote against the Civil Rights Act, and his nomination and forceful defense
of states' rights served to mark a shift in the Republican Party's position
on race, at least in the eyes of many voters. This is why so many scholars
consider 1964 to be the initial, and in many ways defining, year for a
division between the two parties on issues of race.[13] The Democrats finally completed the move started under FDR and established
themselves as fully liberal on the question of race. The Republicans,
under the direction of the conservative wing of the party, moved in
the opposite direction. The party of Lincoln was now clearly the
conservative option on race. Voters had a choice, and it was crystal clear.

If anything, this choice has become even clearer in the years since 1964.
The Democratic Party gradually lost its conservative, southern wing and
the same thing eventually happened with the Republican Party's liberal,
mostly northeastern wing.[14] The eight-year presidency of Ronald Reagan
served to solidify the image of the GOP as conservative on racial issues,
and Reagan's clashes with liberal Democrats in Congress heightened
the distinction between the two parties.[15] Incidents such as the infamous
Willie Horton television ad in the 1988 campaign of Republican presidential candidate George H.W. Bush presented the differences between the
two parties on race in ways that it was almost impossible to miss.[16] Some
argue that the Republican Party has exploited issues surrounding race in
every election cycle since 1964.[17] Still others go further and claim that race
has been *the* dominant cleavage in American electoral politics since the
pivotal year of 1964.[18]

Regardless of whether or not one is willing to go as far as the last two viewpoints in the previous paragraph, it is undeniable that race and ethnicity is now a powerful cleavage within the American electorate. Whites of just about all stripes have become more Republican over the past three decades,[19] while African Americans have been overwhelmingly and steadily Democratic over the same period.[20] Latinos, now the largest racial/ethnic minority in the United States, are also highly Democratic, although not to the degree that African Americans are.[21] Race and ethnicity remain important across a wide array of issues in American politics.[22]

PARTY IMAGES AND THE RACIAL/ETHNIC DIVIDE

So we know there are racial and ethnic differences present in American society in numerous areas, and we also know that the parties take very different positions when it comes to issues related to race and/or ethnicity. We also know that race is an important cleavage in American politics, as Figure 4.1 demonstrates. Dividing the electorate on the basis of whites (non-Latino whites only) and non-whites results in the biggest difference in terms of Democratic presidential vote of any of the four cleavages examined in this study.[23] A majority of whites have voted Democratic for president only once since 1952 (1964, when seemingly everyone voted Democratic), while non-whites have fallen below 70 percent Democratic only once during the same period (66 percent in 1956). Clearly, a major cleavage based on race and ethnicity exists within the American electorate. The more important question for the purposes of this study, however, is whether or not this cleavage manifests itself in terms of party images. Do whites and non-whites see the Republican and Democratic Parties differently?

Beginning with some basics, Figure 4.2 shows that, overall, whites tend to have a higher total number of likes and dislikes than do non-whites. The gap is not terribly large, but it is there and it has increased a bit since the 1980s. This is likely due, at least in part, to the fact that in the U.S. whites on average have higher education levels than do non-whites. And,

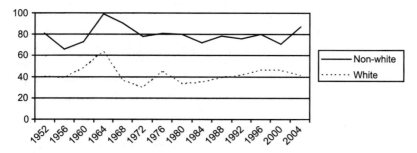

Figure 4.1 Democratic presidential vote by race, 1952–2004.

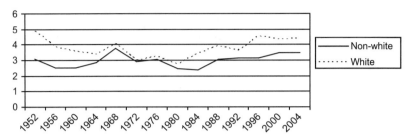

Figure 4.2 Mean party salience (sum of all Democratic and Republican likes and dislikes) by race, 1952–2004.

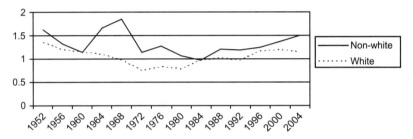

Figure 4.3 Mean number of likes of the Democratic Party by race, 1952–2004.

as we have already seen, higher educational attainment means more party images.

Things get more interesting when we separate out likes from dislikes and Democratic images from Republican ones. Beginning first with likes of the Democratic Party, Figure 4.3 shows that, with two exceptions (ties in 1960 and 1984), non-whites on average have a higher number of likes of the Democratic Party than do whites. This makes sense given the generally sympathetic stands related to minorities and minority issues that the party has routinely taken since 1964. It is worth noting, however, that the gap between non-whites and whites in terms of Democratic likes is not as large as one might suspect it to be, especially since the 1980s. It is also important to point out that both whites and non-whites have seen more to like in the party of Jefferson and Jackson since the mid-1980s.

Staying with the Democrats, Figure 4.4 presents the average number of Democratic dislikes by racial/ethnic group. Here the differences are much more striking. Whites have a higher number of Democratic dislikes than do non-whites, and in most instances the gap is quite large. Whites tend to see the Democratic Party in a more negative light than non-whites. Again, this is not surprising.

Moving to the Republican Party, Figure 4.5 shows the average number of GOP likes by race. Here, once again, we see sizeable differences between racial/ethnic groups. Whites tend to see quite a bit to like about

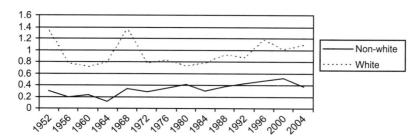

Figure 4.4 Mean number of dislikes of the Democratic Party by race, 1952–2004.

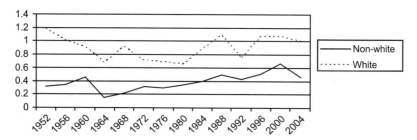

Figure 4.5 Mean number of likes of the Republican Party by race, 1952–2004.

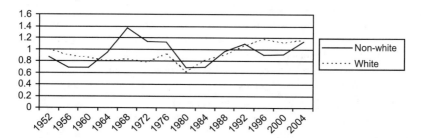

Figure 4.6 Mean number of dislikes of the Republican Party by race, 1952–2004.

the Republicans, while in some years it seems that non-whites struggle to come up with anything nice to say about the party. While it is the case that non-whites have been seeing more that they like about the GOP over the past twenty years, whites are still much more positive about the party on the whole.

While the patterns for the first three likes/dislikes have looked at least somewhat as one would expect, the average number of dislikes of the Republican Party by racial group does not follow suit. As Figure 4.6 demonstrates, with the exception of the four presidential election years from 1964 to 1976, whites have either been equal to or higher than non-whites in their dislikes of the Republicans. This is somewhat surprising, and we will return here later in this chapter. It also bears mentioning that since 1980 the number of dislikes of the Republican Party has risen for both racial/ethnic groups.

While the nature of racial differences in party images is relatively apparent in the data presented thus far, Figure 4.7 really clarifies the differences between whites and non-whites in terms of liking and disliking the two major political parties. In terms of net party affect (remember, this is the sum of Democratic likes and Republican dislikes minus the sum of Democratic dislikes and Republican likes), non-whites tend to be highly pro-Democratic, while whites tend to hover around the neutral line. The distance between the two groups is a bit over 1.5 in 2004, which is a considerable divide.

So there are differences in the likelihood of having positive and negative images of the parties on the basis of race/ethnicity. How are these differences reflected in the substantive nature of the Republican and Democratic images held by non-whites and whites? Table 4.1 presents whites' and non-whites' likes of the Democratic Party by subject area. As we already know, whites are more likely than non-whites to have nothing they like about the Democrats. We also see that for both groups the most common image is rooted in economics. Non-whites tend to be a bit higher than whites here, but both racial groups commonly have a positive image of the Democratic Party based on economics. The percentages within each group liking the Democrats based on party philosophy have also risen since 1980, reflecting the growing salience and importance of ideology in American politics. It is interesting to note that there is generally not much difference here between non-whites and whites. Non-economic domestic images are interesting as well. For whites, non-economic likes of the Democrats were relatively rare until the 1990s, and have risen since then. For non-whites, non-economic domestic images of the Democrats were once quite prevalent (especially at the height of the Civil Rights Movement in the 1960s), but have declined since then (2000 excepted). General party images are relatively common for both racial groups (somewhat higher for non-whites), while the other substantive

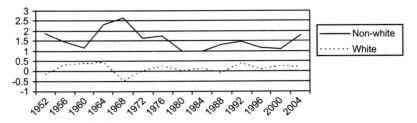

Figure 4.7 Mean net party affect (Democratic likes and Republican dislikes minus Democratic dislikes and Republican likes) by race, 1952–2004.

Table 4.1 Subject area of likes of the Democratic Party by race, 1952–2004

Year	No mention		Economic		Non-economic domestic		Party philosophy		Government management		General party image		People in the party		Foreign policy	
	Non-white	White	Non-white	White	Non-white	White	Non-white	White	Non-white	White	Non-white	White	Non-white	White	Non-white	White
1952	32	38	40	39	10	5	5	6	0	—	8	7	4	4	2	1
1956	40	45	31	32	10	5	1	3	1	0	9	9	8	5	1	0
1960	43	44	38	30	3	5	2	5	2	0	11	12	1	2	0	2
1964	23	44	26	26	22	4	2	4	3	2	14	15	7	3	2	2
1968	19	53	34	20	19	4	4	5	1	2	15	12	7	5	0	1
1972	45	59	30	21	9	3	4	5	—	—	6	8	2	2	2	—
1976	37	58	40	26	4	2	6	5	—	—	8	5	4	2	—	0
1980	42	57	29	20	7	3	9	9	2	—	9	6	2	2	—	—
1984	54	55	21	19	4	3	11	12	0	—	6	7	3	2	—	—
1988	42	53	29	23	4	4	11	11	—	—	10	5	2	1	0	0
1992	42	55	31	20	5	6	12	11	—	—	6	5	1	2	0	0
1996	47	49	25	20	7	11	11	12	—	—	7	6	3	2	0	0
2000	40	45	23	23	12	10	16	12	1	2	6	6	2	2	0	0
2004	34	48	28	19	6	9	17	15	0	1	12	5	1	2	1	1

areas for liking the Democrats fail to generate much of anything from either group.

What about the reasons for disliking the Democratic Party? Table 4.2 provides this information. Again, whites are much more likely than non-whites to have something about the Democrats that rubs them up the wrong way. The most frequent source of irritation among whites is the Democrats' party philosophy. This figure has always been relatively high, is always much higher than the corresponding figure for non-whites, and has grown significantly in recent years. Once again, we see party philosophy hurting the Democrats. General image reasons for disliking the Democratic Party are relatively common for both non-whites and whites, and there is little difference here between the groups. While the percentages are relatively low, whites are clearly more likely to dislike the Democrats on the basis of both economic and non-economic domestic issues. The other substantive categories of a negative image of the Democratic Party are relatively uncommon here for both groups, with the exceptions of foreign policy among whites in 1952 and 1968.

Turning now to the Republican Party, we see again in Table 4.3 that whites are more likely than non-whites to have a positive image of the GOP. More often than any of the other categories, party philosophy is the source of the positive view of the Republicans on the part of whites. This figure has also risen among non-whites over the past few presidential election cycles, but it is still below that exhibited by whites. It should also be noted here that, although the figures are small, higher percentages of whites than non-whites tend to see the Republicans positively for economic, non-economic domestic, and foreign policy reasons. The other categories contain little of interest, with the exception once again of how much whites liked Eisenhower in 1956.

Looking finally at negative images of the Republican Party, we first see in Table 4.4 that—unlike the other three image categories—there is little difference in the likelihood of seeing something that one dislikes about the GOP between the racial/ethnic groups. This is especially true since 1980. There is also little difference between the groups in how they see the Republican Party in terms of economics. Negative images of the GOP rooted in economics are prevalent among both whites and non-whites alike. Dislikes based on party philosophy and non-economic domestic reasons are on the rise, the former among both whites and non-whites while the latter are headed upward mostly among whites. General image dislikes are present in roughly equal measure for both groups, while the other categories do not contain much of interest.

Examining the single most common positive and negative image of each party by race results mostly in the same picture we saw in Chapter 2 when we looked at the electorate as a whole, with one interesting exception. In most years non-whites have so little that they both dislike about the

Table 4.2 Subject area of dislikes of the Democratic Party by race, 1952–2004

Year	No mention		Economic		Non-economic domestic		Party philosophy		Government management		General party image		People in the party		Foreign policy	
	Non-white	White	Non-white	White	Non-white	White	Non-white	White	Non-white	White	Non-white	White	Non-white	White	Non-white	White
1952	81	41	5	11	2	4	1	12	3	12	2	6	2	5	3	10
1956	88	55	1	4	3	4	0	5	1	2	5	13	2	10	1	8
1960	83	61	2	5	4	4	1	11	1	1	4	11	1	3	5	5
1964	90	57	1	4	2	6	2	12	1	5	2	9	0	3	2	4
1968	78	40	1	5	1	5	0	12	2	4	12	17	4	6	2	11
1972	81	57	2	7	1	1	1	12	1	2	9	10	4	8	1	3
1976	81	59	3	7	1	2	4	15	2	4	4	6	2	3	2	4
1980	76	61	7	9	0	2	5	10	2	4	6	8	2	3	2	3
1984	83	59	1	8	0	2	5	14	0	2	5	7	2	4	3	3
1988	77	53	3	10	1	3	6	15	1	5	7	8	2	2	3	3
1992	74	55	3	10	2	4	7	15	4	6	7	6	1	3	1	1
1996	76	47	3	10	2	6	6	20	3	5	8	8	2	1	2	2
2000	72	52	4	6	5	6	6	18	3	4	8	9	2	3	1	2
2004	75	47	0	6	1	7	8	19	3	4	11	12	2	3	1	3

Table 4.3 Subject area of likes of the Republican Party by race, 1952–2004

Year	No mention		Economic		Non-economic domestic		Party philosophy		Government management		General party image		People in the party		Foreign policy	
	Non-white	White	Non-white	White	Non-white	White	Non-white	White	Non-white	White	Non-white	White	Non-white	White	Non-white	White
1952	78	49	7	6	3	2	2	11	0	5	5	11	3	9	1	6
1956	75	47	6	7	7	2	0	6	—	6	3	7	4	18	3	8
1960	71	53	6	6	9	2	0	10	0	3	10	10	0	7	4	9
1964	90	63	2	3	1	2	1	13	0	2	3	8	2	6	0	3
1968	83	53	1	3	2	2	1	15	0	3	4	13	5	6	4	5
1972	80	62	2	4	3	2	—	9	1	3	6	7	5	6	1	6
1976	84	65	2	6	1	1	4	13	—	3	3	5	3	3	3	3
1980	80	64	3	8	1	1	5	10	1	5	5	6	2	3	2	3
1984	79	57	4	2	2	8	3	13	2	3	6	7	2	5	4	5
1988	73	50	6	14	3	3	4	10	2	5	4	6	2	3	6	8
1992	75	62	5	7	3	5	4	11	—	3	5	5	2	3	4	5
1996	78	50	4	8	2	6	7	19	3	7	4	6	1	1	1	2
2000	69	52	6	10	7	8	9	18	2	4	4	5	1	2	2	2
2004	70	51	5	9	3	6	9	16	2	3	7	7	3	2	3	6

Table 4.4 Subject area of dislikes of the Republican Party by race, 1952–2004

Year	No mention		Economic		Non-economic domestic		Party philosophy		Government management		General party image		People in the party		Foreign policy	
	Non-white	White	Non-white	White	Non-white	White	Non-white	White	Non-white	White	Non-white	White	Non-white	White	Non-white	White
1952	53	51	39	28	3	3	1	4	0	0	4	8	1	5	0	2
1956	64	53	23	22	6	7	—	2	0	1	6	6	—	6	0	2
1960	60	54	23	19	6	6	1	5	3	1	8	7	0	2	0	5
1964	44	53	20	15	10	2	1	4	1	2	16	14	9	8	0	2
1968	37	58	27	13	8	2	5	7	1	1	17	12	5	7	0	1
1972	44	58	38	20	2	2	3	4	2	3	6	7	2	3	2	3
1976	47	55	31	20	2	2	5	6	1	2	12	9	2	4	—	2
1980	60	64	22	16	1	3	6	5	1	1	7	7	2	2	0	1
1984	65	59	18	17	4	4	7	7	0	3	3	4	1	2	3	5
1988	56	56	22	19	5	4	4	5	2	4	5	5	—	2	5	5
1992	49	49	29	29	4	4	7	7	2	2	6	6	2	6	2	2
1996	59	46	22	18	5	9	8	11	2	3	3	12	2	2	0	1
2000	58	47	17	18	7	9	8	11	2	4	7	9	1	2	1	1
2004	45	46	22	17	4	9	12	19	3	5	9	10	2	1	3	4

Democratic Party and like about the Republicans that there really is no top image in these categories. Whites, at least since 1964, have a top negative image of the Democrats and a top positive image of the Republicans that is rooted in ideology: liberal for the Democrats and conservative for the Republicans. Among both whites and non-whites the clear top negative image of the GOP is that it is the party of big business and the upper class. These findings all match up with the electorate as a whole. But when we look at the most common positive image of the Democratic Party, a slightly different picture emerges on the basis of race. As Table 4.5 shows, the top reason for whites to like the Democrats is because they see the party as looking out for the interests of the working class, the same as does the electorate as a whole. The top like of non-whites is also rooted in social class, but here the Democratic Party is almost as likely to be seen as the party of the poor and needy in society as it is the party of the working class. This may say something about the economic inequality that still exists among racial and ethnic groups in American society.

CONCLUSION

There are meaningful differences between whites and non-whites in terms of how they see the Republican and Democratic Parties. Overall, non-whites tend to see much more to like about the Democrats, while whites have an easier time seeing something positive about the Republicans. Non-whites tend to have relatively low levels of Democratic dislikes, while whites see much more that they dislike about the Democrats. In an

Table 4.5 Top image for Democratic like by race, 1952–2004

Year	Non-whites	Whites
1952	Bring higher wages and more jobs	Party of working class
1956	Bring higher wages and more jobs	Party of working class
1960	Party of working class	Party of working class
1964	Party of working class	Party of working class
1968	Party of working class	Party of working class
1972	Party of poor and needy people	Party of working class
1976	Party of working class	Party of working class
1980	Party of poor and needy people	Party of working class
1984	Party of poor and needy people	Party of working class
1988	Party of working class and party of poor and needy people (tie)	Party of working class
1992	Party of poor and needy people	Party of working class
1996	Party of working class	Party of working class
2000	Party of working class	Party of working class
2004	Party of poor and needy people	Party of working class

interesting and somewhat unanticipated finding, both whites and non-whites see a fair amount to dislike about the GOP, and they possess these negative images at roughly equal levels.

In terms of the substance behind these images, high percentages of both whites and non-whites like the Democratic Party for economic reasons, although the figure is usually a bit higher on the part of non-whites. Both groups are also increasingly likely to have a positive Democratic Party image rooted in party philosophy. On the flip side, whites are much more likely to dislike the Democrats because of their party philosophy, and the prevalence of this image has been increasing over time among whites. Keeping with party philosophy, whites are much more likely than non-whites to see the Republican Party positively for this reason, and this figure too has been increasing. Finally, both non-whites and whites are quite likely to have negative images of the GOP based on economics. On the whole, we see much the same picture as we have in previous chapters. Economic images are the most common, and they generally tend to advantage the Democrats. However, party philosophy images are increasing in frequency, and these images tend to benefit the Republicans. The twist in this chapter is that party philosophy images are more prevalent among whites than among non-whites.

Chapter 5

Party Images and Sex

We are all familiar with the term "gender gap." It seems that every time an election comes along, especially a presidential election, the media is suddenly awash with talking heads expounding on the gender gap. In case anyone has somehow managed to escape these discussions, the term "gender gap" refers to the difference between women and men in some form of electoral behavior—usually vote choice and party identification, but in some cases other behaviors, such as voter turnout, as well. This chapter will focus solely on vote choice and partisanship. In almost all instances where it is used, the gender gap is presented as the result of women behaving differently from men (although it could just as easily be the other way around with the same result),[1] and contemporary political commentators spend an inordinate amount of time discussing how women are behaving differently from men, and the implications of these behavioral differences.

Over the last thirty years in American politics, the gender gap has referred to the fact that women are more supportive of the Democratic Party than are men. Women are more likely than men to identify as Democrats, and perhaps more important, women are more likely than their male counterparts to vote Democratic at the ballot box. This situation is now so accepted by many political observers that it is almost taken for granted. In many cases it is simply acknowledged as a given that the Democratic candidate will outpoll her or his Republican opponent among women on Election Day; the only question is, by how much? Seemingly everyone agrees that women and men differ politically, and that such differences are natural, part of the normal state of affairs in American politics. Such differences in electoral behavior suggest the possibility of differences in how the sexes see the political parties. The party images of men and women will be the subject of this chapter.

THE "HOWS" AND "WHYS" OF THE GENDER GAP

The media commentators are correct about one thing—the gender gap does exist. As Figure 5.1 shows, women are more Democratic in their vote choice—in this case the presidential vote—than are men. This has been the case in every presidential election since 1964. The distance between men and women grew in the 1980s and has stayed relatively stable since then, with a presidential election high of 13 percentage points in 1996.[2] There is indeed such a thing as the gender gap.

After acknowledging that the gender gap exists, agreement among academics who have studied the phenomenon becomes somewhat harder to come by. One area of disagreement involves the seemingly simple question of timing—when did the gender gap first begin? The most common date of origin given for the gender gap is 1980, and certainly it was the early 1980s when it began to garner attention from the media.[3] Others, however, argue that the gender gap existed before 1980. The mid-1960s is sometimes given as the time of its initial appearance, and some researchers have even made the case for a start date of perhaps as early as the 1950s.[4] Karen Kaufmann presents an analysis that in some ways provides two different relevant dates for the origins of the gender gap. The first is the mid-1960s, when both men and women (whites only) were becoming less Democratic, only men were moving away from the Democrats more rapidly. This difference in defection rate created the initial appearance of the gender gap. Since 1992, however, Kaufmann shows that men and women are moving in opposite directions. Men have continued their shift to the Republican Party, while women are becoming more Democratic. Thus the gender gap has increased.[5] For what it's worth, Henry Kenski likely got it correct when he argued that the gender gap existed prior to 1980, but grew significantly in size after that point.[6]

One of the reasons why 1980 is such an important year, according to many, is because Ronald Reagan won that year's presidential election. Reagan took a very conservative position on certain issues that women

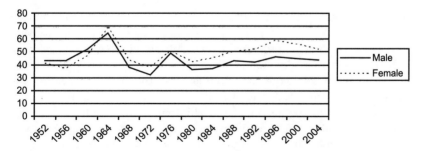

Figure 5.1 Democratic presidential vote by sex, 1952–2004.

were thought to be particularly concerned about—for example, the Equal Rights Amendment and abortion—and at least gave lip service to the desirability of a return to the more traditional family and gender roles that had existed in past American society.[7] In the words of Anne Costain, "By 1980, Ronald Reagan had defeated [Jimmy] Carter and moved the party away from its long-held commitment to equality of the sexes. This helped to establish an antiwoman image of the Republican Party, making the emerging female preference for Democratic candidates and the Democratic Party an enduring gender gap."[8] In this way, the two presidential terms of Ronald Reagan had much the same effect on the gender gap as they did on the electoral cleavage rooted in race and ethnicity discussed in the previous chapter.

At this point we can agree that the gender gap was definitely in existence by the early 1980s and that it grew during that decade, at least in part because of the policy views and actions of Republican President Ronald Reagan. But why was there a gender gap in the first place? What drives women to behave differently from men when it comes to partisanship and vote choice? There are a number of different answers to that question.

Perhaps the earliest theory to emerge for the cause of the gender gap had to do with compassion—specifically the claim that women were more compassionate than men. In the words of Carol Gilligan, whose book, *In a Different Voice*, was largely responsible for generating the compassion theory, "The moral imperative that emerges repeatedly in interviews with women is an injunction to care, a responsibility to discern and alleviate the 'real and recognizable' trouble of this world."[9] Because women were more likely than men to care about the problems of others, they were more likely to support the party that looked out for and tried to assist the less fortunate as opposed to the party that stressed individualism and taking care of one's own problems. In other words, women were more likely to support the Democrats.[10]

While not dismissing the compassion argument, other researchers emphasized that there was a far more tangible reason why women were more supportive of government efforts to help the less advantaged and were thus more Democratic than men. Women, according to this argument, were more supportive of state efforts to help the disadvantaged because women were much more likely to find themselves in the disadvantaged category some day than were men. Simply put, women were more likely to be economically vulnerable than men, and thus were more likely to identify with and vote for candidates of the party advocating the stronger social safety net—the Democrats.[11] The increases in the number of divorces and in the percentage of children born outside of marriage changed the family structure in America, and more often than not it was women who came out on the short end of the stick.[12] Women recognized this and did the sensible thing politically—they shifted their electoral behavior toward the party most likely to help them if they should indeed find themselves in a position of vulnerability.

Other researchers looked to the coercive power of the state for answers to the causes of the gender gap. They found that women were much less supportive of state-sanctioned and state-conducted violence in a variety of forms—capital punishment, aggressive foreign policy (the threat of violence), and use of military force. Because women were less supportive of state violence, they were more likely to support the party seen as less aggressive and less likely to use force or violence. Since 1980, that party has been the Democrats, and thus the gender gap is explained.[13]

Still other researchers have turned away from compassion, economic vulnerability, and violence for insight into the gender gap and have turned toward cultural issues. For this explanation, women tend to be more liberal on many of the hot-button issues that make up the ongoing culture war in American politics.[14] According to this view, it is issues such as abortion, the Equal Rights Amendment and women's rights overall, civil rights for homosexuals and other minorities, etc., that fuel the gender gap. Women are more liberal than men on these cultural issues, and thus they tend to side more than men with the culturally liberal party—the Democratic Party.[15] Taking this argument to perhaps its natural conclusion, Pamela Johnston Conover argues that it is solely feminists who are responsible for the gender gap rather than all women as a group.[16]

PARTY IMAGES AND SEX

It is doubtful that the debate outlined above over the causes of the gender gap will be settled any time soon. It is likely that all of the causes noted in the previous paragraphs have some bearing on the gender gap, as some scholars have pointed out.[17] Fortunately, for our purposes, the causation behind the gender gap does not really matter all that much. What we are concerned with is whether or not women and men see the Republican and Democratic Parties differently. As was the case in previous chapters, in order for party images to differ based on the different political concerns of men and women, the parties have to take positions on these issues that are somewhat opposed to each other, and they have to publicize these positions. Once again, this condition is easily satisfied. As was alluded to at a number of points already in this chapter, the Democrats and Republicans take opposing stands on all of the issues we have discussed in the course of this chapter as possible contributors to the gender gap. The Republicans routinely argue for increased self-reliance and a reduction in the social welfare state, while the Democrats argue for programs to assist the less fortunate and an expansion of the social safety net. The Democrats, at least since 1980, have been less aggressive in foreign policy and more likely to pursue non-military solutions to problems, while the GOP has been much more aggressive and more willing to use the force of the American military. On cultural issues, the Republicans are conservative almost across the board, while the Democrats are much more liberal.[18] So the parties do indeed differ on issues that might make gender a relevant factor in Americans' party images. The question, then, is whether or not this happens. What do the data tell us?

Figure 5.2 presents the mean number of total party likes and dislikes for women and for men. In an unexpected finding, men have a higher number of total likes and dislikes than do women for all years examined here. Since the 1980s, this margin has actually increased in size, with men having somewhere from around 1 to 1.5 more combined partisan likes and dislikes.

Separating out party images by likes and dislikes and by party, Figure 5.3 shows the mean number of Democratic likes by sex. Here we see very little difference between men and women. Indeed, in the last three presidential election years women and men have been virtually the same in their average number of likes of the Democratic Party. The number of Democratic likes has also increased for both sexes since 1980, mirroring a trend that we have seen in previous chapters. Looking at dislikes of the Democratic Party, however, presents a different picture. Here men and women differ significantly, as Figure 5.4 demonstrates. Men have seen

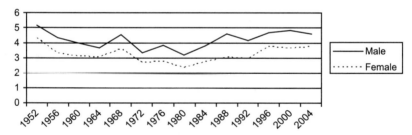

Figure 5.2 Mean party salience (sum of all Democratic and Republican likes and dislikes) by sex, 1952–2004.

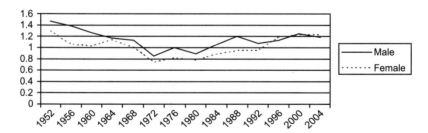

Figure 5.3 Mean number of likes of the Democratic Party by sex, 1952–2004.

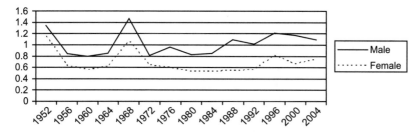

Figure 5.4 Mean number of dislikes of the Democratic Party by sex, 1952–2004.

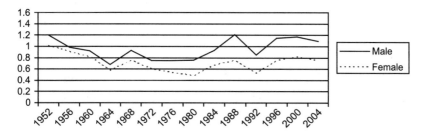

Figure 5.5 Mean number of likes of the Republican Party by sex, 1952–2004.

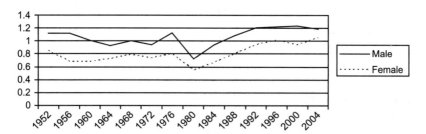

Figure 5.6 Mean number of dislikes of the Republican Party by sex, 1952–2004.

more to dislike about the Democrats than have women every presidential election year since 1972, and this divide has increased over time. Both men and women are more likely now to see something unappealing about the Democratic Party than they were in the early 1970s, but the rate of increase has been higher among men.

Looking at likes of the Republican Party continues the theme of differences between the sexes. Here, as can be seen in Figure 5.5, men have a higher average number of Republican Party likes than do women. This has been true in every year examined here, but the distance between men and women started to rise in 1972. Both sexes have seen more to like in the GOP since that time, but once again men have been increasing their Republican likes at a much higher rate than have women. Figure 5.6, presenting dislikes of the Republican Party, in some ways represents a middle ground between the Democratic likes trend in Figure 5.3 and the Democratic dislikes and Republican likes trends shown in Figures 5.4 and 5.5. In Figure 5.3 we see that men, on average, see more to dislike about the Republicans than do women. However, the average GOP dislikes move in almost the exact same pattern for women and for men. Indeed, both sexes have seen a relatively steep increase in their dislikes of the Republican Party since 1980, and in 2004 men and women were as close as they have ever been in terms of GOP dislikes in this entire time series.

So how does this all look when we turn, as we always do at this point in a chapter, to the issue of net affect? Figure 5.7 presents these results, and here it is clear that the Democratic Party fares much better among women than among men, and that this has been the case since the early 1980s. In the 1960s and 1970s, the net party affect was roughly the same for men and for women—moving up and down in almost the same fashion for both sexes. Since 1980 this has changed dramatically. Women have moved in a much more positive Democratic direction in terms of net affect, while men have stayed relatively stable at a point somewhere between neutral and slightly pro-Democratic (1992 excepted). The net affect results lend support for both the 1980 start date for the gender gap and the importance of Ronald Reagan in clarifying party differences based on sex.

Turning next to the substance behind these images, Table 5.1 presents the positive images of the Democratic Party by subject area for men and for women. In a repeat of what we saw in terms of the number of Democratic likes among women and men, we see little difference between the sexes in terms of why they like the Democrats. No matter where one looks in Table 5.1, there fails to be much of a difference between the guys and the gals. Positive images of the Democrats rooted in economics are the most common image for both sexes, and positive views of the party based on non-economic domestic issues and party philosophy have grown in both groups as well. We see that the philosophy image growth began in the 1980s, while the non-economic domestic growth first appeared in the 1990s.

We see greater differences between the sexes in Table 5.2 which presents the negatives images of the Democratic Party by subject area. Once again,

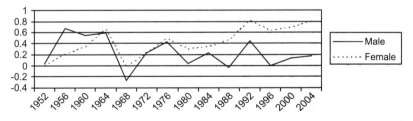

Figure 5.7 Mean net party affect (Democratic likes and Republican dislikes minus Democratic dislikes and Republican likes) by sex, 1952–2004.

Table 5.1 Subject area of likes of the Democratic Party by sex, 1952–2004

Year	No mention		Economic		Non-economic domestic		Party philosophy		Government management		General party image		People in the party		Foreign policy	
	Male	Female	Male	Female	Male	Female	Male	Female	Male	Female	Male	Female	Male	Female	Male	Female
1952	33	41	42	36	6	5	7	4	0	–	6	8	3	4	2	1
1956	37	50	38	27	5	6	4	2	0	0	8	9	6	5	1	0
1960	38	48	33	28	5	4	7	3	1	0	11	13	2	2	2	1
1964	41	41	27	25	6	6	5	2	2	3	13	16	3	4	2	2
1968	46	52	25	19	6	6	6	4	2	–	11	13	5	4	0	–
1972	55	59	24	21	3	3	7	4	–	–	7	8	2	3	2	–
1976	50	58	29	27	3	2	8	4	2	–	5	6	3	3	–	0
1980	49	58	25	19	4	4	10	8	2	–	6	7	3	2	–	–
1984	51	58	22	17	3	4	13	11	–	–	6	7	3	2	–	–
1988	47	54	26	24	5	4	14	9	–	–	6	6	–	2	–	–
1992	49	54	26	20	6	5	11	12	–	–	5	5	–	2	0	0
1996	47	50	21	21	11	10	11	12	–	–	8	5	–	3	0	0
2000	44	44	23	23	11	10	15	12	2	2	4	7	2	2	0	–
2004	46	47	22	19	8	9	13	16	2	0	7	7	2	1	–	1

Table 5.2 Subject area of dislikes of the Democratic Party by sex, 1952–2004

Year	No mention		Economic		Non-economic domestic		Party philosophy		Government management		General party image		People in the party		Foreign policy	
	Male	Female	Male	Female	Male	Female	Male	Female	Male	Female	Male	Female	Male	Female	Male	Female
1952	39	50	11	9	4	3	13	9	12	10	6	5	5	5	10	9
1956	53	62	4	4	4	3	6	3	3	1	11	12	10	8	8	6
1960	57	68	6	4	4	3	13	8	1	0	10	10	3	2	7	4
1964	55	65	4	3	7	5	14	9	6	4	8	8	3	2	4	3
1968	38	49	6	3	5	4	13	9	5	3	16	17	6	6	12	9
1972	54	64	8	5	2	1	11	9	2	2	12	9	9	7	3	3
1976	54	69	9	5	2	1	16	11	5	3	6	6	4	2	5	3
1980	56	70	11	7	2	1	12	7	5	3	8	7	4	3	3	3
1984	57	70	9	6	2	2	15	10	3	1	8	5	4	3	4	3
1988	47	68	12	6	3	3	18	9	6	3	8	7	2	2	4	3
1992	50	68	12	5	4	3	17	10	7	5	7	6	3	2	2	1
1996	48	60	11	6	5	6	21	13	5	4	7	9	1	1	2	2
2000	46	66	8	4	8	4	18	12	3	4	10	7	3	2	3	1
2004	47	60	7	2	7	4	18	15	5	4	11	11	3	2	3	2

note that men have more that they dislike about the Democrats than do women. Men's biggest gripe with the Democrats has to do with party philosophy. This dislike has been growing among women as well, but the figures are still higher among men. Men are also more likely to have negative images of the Democrats rooted in both economic and non-economic domestic issues than are women, and we also see that men tend to pay a bit more attention to how the Democrats undertake government management.

Moving to the Republican Party images, we see immediately in Table 5.3 that men are more likely to have a positive image of the GOP than are women. The most common source of this positive view among men is the Republicans' party philosophy, although this has grown among women as well. Men are also more likely to see the Republicans positively for economic reasons than are women. This image has increased among men in recent years, lending some support to both the compassion and welfare state arguments for the existence of the gender gap discussed earlier in this chapter. We also see, for the first time in this analysis, foreign policy making up an important component of a party's image. Although it does not show up in all years, there are a number of years here in which men see the Republican Party positively as a result of foreign policy. The figures here for men are always higher than they are for women (1952 excepted), thus lending some support to the explanation of the gender gap rooted in military usage and violence issues. Finally, it is worth pointing out that positive non-economic domestic images of the GOP have grown slightly among both sexes, but that they have grown more among men.

While positive Republican images presented a picture of difference between the sexes, negative images of the GOP display greater similarity (see Table 5.4). Negative Republican images rooted in economics are the top choice for both men and women, and have been throughout the entire period under examination here. Negative views of the party based on party philosophy and non-economic domestic issues have been increasing among both women and men, with men slightly more likely to see the GOP in a negative light because of party philosophy.

Looking at the top individual party likes and dislikes by sex reveals almost identical results on the part of men and women, and also the same pattern seen in the general electorate. For both sexes the most common reason for liking the Democratic Party is because it is the party of the working class, while the most common reason for disliking the Republicans is because they are seen as the party of big business and the upper class. This is the case in every presidential election year from 1952 through 2004. Since 1964, the top positive image of the GOP is the party's conservatism or some variant of conservative ideology, while women and men both have top Democratic dislikes tied to liberal ideology over the same period.

Table 5.3 Subject area of likes of the Republican Party by sex, 1952–2004

Year	No mention		Economic		Non-economic domestic		Party philosophy		Government management		General party image		People in the party		Foreign policy	
	Male	Female	Male	Female	Male	Female	Male	Female	Male	Female	Male	Female	Male	Female	Male	Female
1952	47	56	7	6	2	2	12	8	6	4	10	11	11	7	5	6
1956	48	51	6	7	3	2	7	4	6	5	5	7	17	16	8	7
1960	51	58	8	5	4	1	12	8	3	2	8	11	6	7	10	8
1964	62	68	3	3	3	2	16	9	2	1	7	8	5	6	3	2
1968	52	61	4	3	3	2	16	12	3	2	13	11	5	6	5	5
1972	62	67	6	3	2	2	10	7	2	2	6	8	3	6	7	5
1976	62	73	8	4	2	1	14	10	4	2	4	5	3	2	5	2
1980	69	75	5	3	0	–	11	9	5	2	6	5	5	3	2	1
1984	55	67	9	6	1	2	13	9	3	3	7	7	3	3	6	4
1988	47	63	16	10	3	3	11	7	5	4	6	5	3	3	11	5
1992	58	71	10	4	6	3	11	8	3	3	5	5	2	2	6	4
1996	49	63	8	7	5	5	20	13	7	5	7	5	–	1	3	1
2000	47	63	11	7	9	6	18	14	5	3	5	5	2	2	3	1
2004	46	62	11	5	6	4	16	12	4	2	7	8	3	2	8	3

Table 5.4 Subject area of dislikes of the Republican Party by sex, 1952–2004

Year	No mention		Economic		Non-economic domestic		Party philosophy		Government management		General party image		People in the party		Foreign policy	
	Male	Female	Male	Female	Male	Female	Male	Female	Male	Female	Male	Female	Male	Female	Male	Female
1952	44	56	33	25	3	3	6	2	0	0	6	8	5	3	2	2
1956	44	61	27	19	8	6	3	1	1	1	6	6	7	5	3	1
1960	46	62	21	18	7	5	7	2	2	1	9	6	2	2	6	4
1964	47	56	17	14	3	3	6	3	2	2	15	13	8	8	1	1
1968	50	59	15	14	3	2	8	6	1	1	13	12	8	5	1	1
1972	52	60	25	20	2	2	5	3	4	2	6	7	3	2	3	3
1976	46	60	25	18	3	1	8	5	2	2	10	9	4	4	3	1
1980	57	68	20	15	2	3	7	4	1	1	9	5	2	3	1	1
1984	54	66	19	15	4	4	8	6	3	3	5	2	2	2	5	3
1988	49	61	22	17	5	4	7	4	6	3	5	4	2	2	5	5
1992	44	54	26	21	5	6	10	7	6	2	5	6	2	2	2	1
1996	45	52	19	19	7	8	11	9	4	2	9	9	4	1	0	1
2000	43	55	20	17	9	8	12	8	4	3	10	7	2	1	1	0
2004	43	51	17	19	7	8	12	8	5	4	11	7	2	1	4	3

CONCLUSION

On the whole, we see that there are both similarities and differences in how men and women see the two major political parties in the United States. On the one hand, women and men are quite similar in having positive images of the Democratic Party rooted in economics and to a lesser extent party philosophy and non-economic domestic issues, and also in possessing negative images of the Republican Party for much the same reasons that they liked the Democrats. On the other hand, men and women differ significantly in their negative images of the Democrats and their positive images of the Republicans. Men are more likely to see the Democrats negatively, due in large part to party philosophy but also increasingly on the bases of economics and non-economic domestic issues. Men are also much more likely than women to have a positive image of the Republican Party, again primarily because of party philosophy but also increasingly because of economics and, in some years, foreign policy.

The bottom line is that there are both important similarities and differences in how women and men see American political parties. It is likely that the differences contribute at least somewhat to the gender gap. We will return to this matter in the final chapter. For now we move on to the final cleavage to be examined in this study—religious salience.

Chapter 6

Party Images and Religious Salience

For at least the last three presidential elections, one cannot delve too far into the post-election analysis without hearing or reading some variant of the following statement: "The biggest factor in how a person voted on Tuesday was whether or not that person was in church on Sunday [or Friday or Saturday]." One almost gets the impression that instead of spending millions of dollars on sophisticated polls and focus groups, those interested in determining how an election is going to play out would be better off simply determining how many voters were in attendance at worship services across the nation the weekend prior to Election Day.

Predicting elections, of course, is not that simple, and no single voter characteristic alone—not even party identification—is powerful enough to determine individual vote choice in and of itself. However, the point behind the high level of attention now being devoted to church attendance is that how much religion matters to a person now matters in American elections. "The importance of religion to the individual"[1]—referred to in this study as religious salience but also called religiosity or religious commitment—is now thought to be a powerful determinant of individuals' electoral behavior, and also the source of a major cleavage within the American electorate. As such, it is certainly possible that religious salience also affects the images that Americans have of their political parties. This chapter examines this possibility.

RISING IMPORTANCE OF RELIGIOUS SALIENCE

Religion as being of importance in American politics is, of course, not a new development or unique phenomenon. The divide between Catholics and Protestants dominated American politics (outside of the South) in the post-bellum nineteenth century; it was critical in the formation of the New Deal coalition, and remained relevant at least through the 1960s.[2] But historically religion has affected electoral politics in the United States along denominational or religious tradition lines. Under a cleavage rooted in religious salience, on the other hand, denominations and religious traditions are relatively meaningless. All that matters is how important religion—regardless of what that religion is—is to the individual. If religion is very important, the person in question is likely to behave politically in a certain fashion; if religion is largely irrelevant to that person, she or he will then act politically in a very different way. We know that religion retains an importance in the United States that is highly unusual compared to other Western nations, so the existence of a political cleavage rooted in religious salience makes a good deal of sense.[3]

For most chroniclers of the subject, the rise of religious salience to political prominence has its roots in the growing importance of cultural issues in American politics. We see the beginnings of this development in the early 1960s when, in successive years, the Supreme Court issued decisions banning prayer (*Engel v. Vitale*, 370 U.S. 421 (1962)) and Bible reading (*Abington School District v. Schempp*, 374 U.S. 203 (1963)) in public schools. Both practices were widespread in the United States at the time, and in many ways served as a first notice to religiously and culturally conservative Americans that change was on the way.[4] Other developments soon pushed cultural issues further up the political agenda. The latter years of the 1960s saw the flowering of a sexual revolution in the United States that advocated higher levels of promiscuity and sex outside of marriage and greater acceptance of homosexuality.[5] The second wave of the women's movement also came to the forefront in the 1960s, with at least in some instances a much more strident form of feminism.[6] Out-of-wedlock births, births to teenage mothers, and divorce were all skyrocketing.[7] By the time the Supreme Court legalized abortion with its decision in *Roe v. Wade* (410 U.S. 113 (1973)), it was clear that cultural issues would soon assume a prominent place in America's public dialogue.[8]

Robert Wuthnow was one of the first scholars to note how the increasing importance of cultural issues was affecting American society. Wuthnow believed that the rise to prominence of issues such as school prayer, pornography, abortion, and gay rights was increasingly dividing Americans into two camps, which he labeled the "religiously liberal" and the "religiously conservative." According to Wuthnow, religious liberals were in favor of removing religion from schools, were tolerant of sexual content in the marketplace, and supportive of abortion rights and homosexual rights. Religious conservatives took the opposite positions on these issues.[9] James Davison Hunter echoed the claims of Wuthnow, and argued that this division was becoming increasingly relevant in the political realm. As Hunter famously phrased it, "America is in the midst of a culture war that has and will continue to have reverberations not only within public policy, but within the lives of ordinary Americans everywhere."[10] Hunter labeled the combatants in this culture war orthodox and progressive, and centered the fundamental difference between the two sides on different sources of moral authority. Again, quoting from Hunter, "The nub of political disagreement today . . . can be traced ultimately and finally to the matter of moral authority. By moral authority I mean the basis by which people determine whether something is good or bad, right or wrong, acceptable or unacceptable, and so on."[11]

This is where religious salience comes in. According to Hunter, those on the orthodox side of the culture war placed ultimate moral authority in a higher power, usually God. Right and wrong were clear, and always the same. What is right for one person is also right for another and what was right fifty years ago is still right today, because God clearly established right and wrong and also clearly differentiated between the two. For Hunter's progressives, right and wrong were subjective matters. They were rooted in rationality and science. Right and wrong were relative to both time and the individual human experience.[12] In other words, we each decide for ourselves what is right and what is wrong. It is not too much of a leap to expect most of those for whom religion is very important to line up on the orthodox side, while those with low levels of religious salience set up camp on the progressive side of this divide.

The arguments of Wuthnow and Hunter received a good deal of attention, and became the source of much additional research. The early results of this research were mixed, finding some division of the religiously conservative and the religiously liberal on abortion and some family-related issues, but not much else.[13] As time went on, however, more and more research did begin to find that Americans were becoming increasingly divided by cultural issues such as abortion, sexual morality, school prayer, and gay rights.[14] Additional research found that these differences were beginning to show up in the political realm as well. There was a dramatic increase in the number of Americans who felt that family decline—a central cultural issue—was the biggest problem facing the United States, and that how voters saw the issue of family decline was increasingly affecting vote choice.[15] Geoffrey Layman demonstrated that the elites of the Democratic and Republican Parties were becoming increasingly different from each other on issues such as gay rights, abortion, and women's rights, and also that individuals' views on these issues were increasingly affecting electoral behavior at the mass level.[16] Views on abortion, regarded by many as the most important cultural issues, were shown to have an especially powerful effect on partisanship and vote choice.[17] While all of these findings certainly point to the possibility of a rise in the impact of religious salience in the political arena, this increase was demonstrated convincingly when a number of works demonstrated convincingly that the effect of religious salience on individual partisanship and vote choice had indeed grown significantly since the early 1990s.[18] Figure 6.1 provides one example of this increase, showing the increasing divide since 1992 in

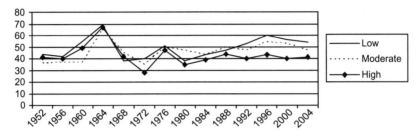

Figure 6.1 Democratic presidential vote by church attendance, 1952–2004.

the Democratic presidential vote on the basis of frequency of church attendance. Today, the less one goes to church the more likely one is to vote Democratic for president. This was not true before the 1990s.

CULTURAL ISSUES, RELIGIOUS SALIENCE, AND THE POLITICAL PARTIES

As has been said repeatedly in this book, no matter how important an issue or set of issues are, they cannot become relevant politically unless the political parties adopt differing positions on these issues. Once again, the Democrats and Republicans have been very accommodating on this front when it comes to cultural issues and religious salience. These differences did not emerge overnight. Indeed, as cultural issues first appeared and grew in strength in the 1960s and 1970s, both parties were somewhat reluctant to engage these issues and were purposively ambiguous about where they stood. By the 1980s, such reluctance and ambiguity was long gone, once again due in no small part to the clarifying impact of Ronald Reagan. The Republican Party was now clearly the party opposed to abortion, less supportive of homosexual rights, in favor of a prominent place for religion in the public square, and more concerned with the state of the family in American society. The Democratic Party proudly presented itself as the defender of women's reproductive freedom, the champion of equality for gays and lesbians, advocate of a high wall of separation between church and state, and supporter of a variety of familial arrangements in addition to the traditional nuclear family unit. Those for whom religion was highly salient became a—some would say the—key element of the Republican base, while low and no salience voters became crucial elements within the Democratic Party.[19] We are now clearly in a situation where Americans of differing levels of religious salience could very well see the parties differently. Is this the case?

PARTY IMAGES AND RELIGIOUS SALIENCE

Following the established pattern, we will begin with some basics. Religious salience in this analysis will be measured using church attendance. Admittedly church attendance by itself is a less than ideal measure of religious salience. As is commonly pointed out, religious salience is a multifaceted phenomenon and, at the very least, should be measured using both a behavioral and attitudinal component.[20] Unfortunately, the only religious salience measure available in the ANES throughout the entire period of this study is church attendance. In 1980 the ANES did introduce a religious guidance measure, which serves as a useful attitudinal measure of religious salience. But it does not go back in time long enough for use here.[21]

Figure 6.2 presents the mean party salience by low, moderate, and high levels of church attendance.[22] In a, by now, familiar pattern, we see that the frequency of partisan likes and dislikes bottomed out for all three attendance levels in 1980, and has risen steadily for all three since then. We also see that there is very little difference in the mean party salience by frequency of church attendance. Indeed, there is a virtual tie among all three groups for every year in this analysis.

What happens when we move to likes and dislikes separately by party? Figure 6.3 demonstrates that there is not much difference between low,

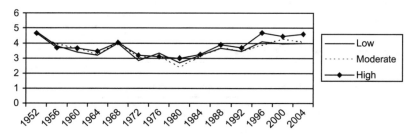

Figure 6.2 Mean party salience (sum of all Democratic and Republican likes and dislikes) by church attendance, 1952–2004.

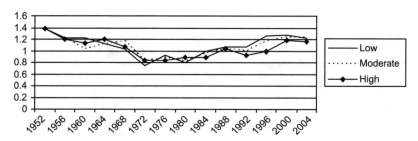

Figure 6.3 Mean number of likes of the Democratic Party by church attendance, 1952–2004.

moderate, and high church attendance groups in terms of the average number of Democratic likes. The number of Democratic likes has risen for all
three groups since 1980, and the only real difference between the groups
occurs in 1996 when low attenders have a slightly higher mean than do
high attenders. But even this is small compared to many of the other
differences we have seen thus far. A look at Democratic dislikes—presented in Figure 6.4—provides a little more contrast between the groups.
Until the end of the 1980s, there was not much difference between the
groups in their mean dislikes of the Democratic Party. This began to
change in 1992, and there is now a sizeable gap between high attenders on
one hand and low and moderate attenders on the other. Those who attend
worship services on a regular basis now have a higher number of dislikes
than those who attend at a less than regular level. This is supportive of
differences in party images based on religious salience.

The averages on likes of the Republican Party presented in Figure 6.5
are also supportive of salience-based image distinctions. Here we see a
pattern of Republican likes rising as church attendance rises. High attenders have the most GOP likes, low attenders the lowest number, and those
who attend worship services at the moderate level are in between the
two. This trend begins in 1980, and has increased in magnitude since.
However, Figure 6.6—showing the average number of Republican dislikes

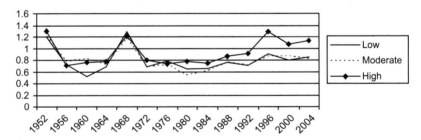

Figure 6.4 Mean number of dislikes of the Democratic Party by church attendance,
1952–2004.

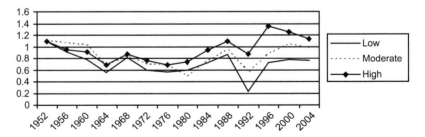

Figure 6.5 Mean number of likes of the Republican Party by church attendance, 1952–
2004.

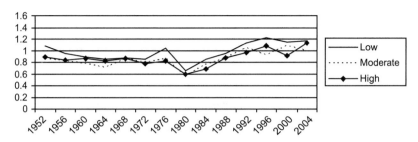

Figure 6.6 Mean number of dislikes of the Republican Party by church attendance, 1952–2004.

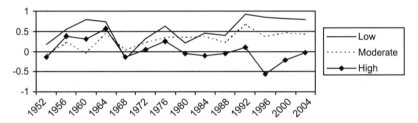

Figure 6.7 Mean net party affect (Democratic likes and Republican dislikes minus Democratic dislikes and Republican likes) by church attendance, 1952–2004.

by attendance level—brings us back to a picture of less distinction. Here there is very little difference in the number of GOP dislikes by attendance level. The three lines move almost in lockstep, and while there has been a bit of spread since 1992, the movement is jumbled enough to prevent any meaningful interpretation.

The net party affect results have provided increased clarity in previous chapters, and that is also the case here. As Figure 6.7 clearly demonstrates, the distance between low attenders and high attenders in net party affect has really grown since 1988. Low attenders have moved in a much more positive net Democratic direction, while higher attenders are now either neutral or in the pro-GOP camp. The results presented here offer the most support yet for differences in party images rooted in religious salience levels.

Shifting to the subject areas of the partisan likes and dislikes by level of church attendance, Table 6.1 presents the likes of the Democratic Party by subject. There really is little difference by attendance level in this table. The groups are about equal in having something they like about the Democrats, and economics remains the number one like of the party for all three levels of attendance throughout the entire time period. Likes of the Democrats based on party philosophy have risen for all three levels, and are just about equal across the groups. The only item of possible

Table 6.1 Subject area of likes of the Democratic Party by church attendance, 1952–2004

Year	No mention			Economic			Non-economic domestic			Party philosophy			Government management			General party image			People in the party			Foreign policy		
	L	M	H	L	M	H	L	M	H	L	M	H	L	M	H	L	M	H	L	M	H	L	M	H
1952	38	37	37	38	38	40	5	6	6	6	6	6	1	0	0	6	8	8	4	4	2	1	1	2
1956	44	50	42	34	24	34	5	5	7	4	2	3	0	0	0	7	11	9	6	7	5	0	—	1
1960	44	49	42	29	29	31	4	4	5	4	4	5	1	1	0	12	11	13	3	2	2	2	2	2
1964	43	43	40	26	24	27	4	7	8	4	3	3	2	2	3	16	15	13	3	4	5	2	2	2
1968	52	42	49	21	24	22	4	7	7	6	4	4	—	3	3	11	15	12	5	4	5	1	0	0
1972	60	57	52	21	23	25	3	4	4	5	5	6	—	1	1	6	8	9	3	1	3	2	—	—
1976	54	53	57	28	28	28	2	3	2	6	6	4	—	2	0	5	6	5	3	2	3	0	0	—
1980	55	54	53	21	22	23	3	4	4	9	9	7	2	—	—	6	7	9	3	2	2	—	—	—
1984	55	54	56	19	19	21	3	5	3	13	11	11	0	—	—	6	8	7	3	2	2	—	—	—
1988	53	50	47	24	21	29	4	5	5	11	13	9	—	—	—	5	9	7	1	—	3	—	—	—
1992	52	50	54	20	26	24	7	6	3	13	11	10	—	—	—	5	4	6	2	2	2	—	0	0
1996	45	47	56	21	24	19	12	10	8	12	12	9	—	—	0	7	5	6	2	2	—	0	0	0
2000	45	43	43	24	19	25	9	12	10	14	16	10	2	2	2	4	6	8	3	2	1	0	0	0
2004	48	45	44	17	25	23	12	5	6	14	16	14	1	0	1	5	7	9	2	1	2	2	1	—

interest in terms of group differences in Table 6.1 lies in the non-economic domestic category. Here we see a rise among all three levels beginning in the 1990s, and in two of the last three presidential election years low attenders have been more likely than high attenders to have such a positive image of the Democrats. However, this pattern did not exist in 2000, which means this might just be an anomaly. It will be interesting to see what develops here in the future.

The substantive areas of dislikes for the Democratic Party, presented in Table 6.2, demonstrate a bit more differentiation on the basis of church attendance, but still not as much as we have seen for some of the other cleavages examined previously. As noted earlier, we see that high church attenders are more likely to have something that they dislike about the Democrats, and the primary source of that negative image has to do with party philosophy. This is also true for moderate and low attenders, and while the negative party philosophy image is higher for high attenders (as we would expect for a difference based on salience), the gap is usually not that large. Perhaps the most interesting finding in Table 6.2 is the growing dislike based on non-economic domestic issues of the Democrats among high attenders. This is certainly supportive of a salience image in party images.

Such a view is reinforced when one examines the likes of the Republican Party by subject area, presented in Table 6.3. High attenders are generally more likely to see something they like about the GOP than are those who attend at moderate and especially low levels. They also tend to like the Republicans more for party philosophy reasons than do their moderate- and low-attending counterparts. But the figure that jumps out most from Table 6.3 is the growth in positive Republican images rooted in non-economic issues among the high attenders. Since 1992 high attenders are much more likely than those in the other two groups to see the GOP positively because of non-economic domestic issues. This is supportive of image differentiation based on religious salience.

Looking finally at the substantive areas of Republican Party dislikes in Table 6.4, we see the three groups as being roughly even in having something they dislike about the party. The most common dislike for all groups in all years (with the exception of moderate attenders in 1968) is economic, and these figures are roughly equal across years and attendance groups. The percentages disliking the Republicans for party philosophy have risen, again roughly equally for all three attendance levels. Negative non-economic domestic images have also risen among all groups since 1992, and in 1996 and 2000 the presence of these images was virtually the same for all three levels of attendance. This changed in 2004, with low attenders having more than double the negative non-economic domestic GOP images of high attenders. Obviously one year does not a pattern make, but this is an interesting development to watch for in future years.

Table 6.2 Subject area of dislikes of the Democratic Party by church attendance, 1952–2004

Year	No mention			Economic			Non-economic domestic			Party philosophy			Government management			General party image			People in the party			Foreign policy		
	L	M	H	L	M	H	L	M	H	L	M	H	L	M	H	L	M	H	L	M	H	L	M	H
1952	46	49	44	10	10	10	4	3	3	10	11	11	10	12	12	6	6	5	6	2	5	10	8	9
1956	59	57	58	4	3	4	3	5	4	5	6	4	2	2	2	13	11	12	9	13	8	7	4	8
1960	67	57	61	4	7	5	3	4	4	7	17	11	1	1	1	11	5	12	2	4	2	6	5	4
1964	61	61	60	4	3	4	8	6	4	10	11	13	4	4	5	9	9	8	2	2	3	3	2	4
1968	44	48	44	6	3	3	5	4	5	9	13	12	4	4	3	17	14	17	6	6	6	11	9	10
1972	61	60	57	5	8	8	1	2	1	10	9	11	2	2	1	11	9	10	7	7	9	3	2	3
1976	61	63	63	6	7	6	1	2	2	12	15	14	4	3	5	8	4	5	4	2	2	4	4	4
1980	63	69	61	9	8	9	1	1	2	9	6	13	4	3	4	8	8	6	3	3	3	3	3	2
1984	63	67	63	8	6	6	2	2	4	12	11	13	2	1	2	7	5	6	4	3	2	3	4	4
1988	59	62	57	9	9	8	2	3	5	12	10	15	4	5	3	8	6	7	2	2	2	3	4	2
1992	61	60	55	8	6	10	2	3	6	12	13	16	6	6	4	7	7	6	3	2	2	1	2	1
1996	57	58	44	8	9	8	2	6	9	16	11	24	6	3	4	8	10	7	1	0	2	2	2	1
2000	60	57	52	6	6	5	5	6	8	13	16	17	3	3	4	9	8	9	2	3	4	2	1	1
2004	56	56	49	5	4	5	3	7	8	16	17	17	4	3	4	11	9	13	3	3	2	4	1	1

Table 6.3 Subject area of likes of the Republican Party by church attendance, 1952–2004

Year	No mention			Economic			Non-economic domestic			Party philosophy			Government management			General party image			People in the party			Foreign policy		
	L	M	H	L	M	H	L	M	H	L	M	H	L	M	H	L	M	H	L	M	H	L	M	H
1952	54	53	50	5	8	6	2	2	3	10	9	11	5	6	4	10	11	12	10	6	8	4	5	6
1956	51	50	47	7	6	7	2	3	2	4	6	6	7	6	5	6	5	7	15	18	17	7	6	9
1960	58	47	54	7	7	5	2	4	2	8	11	11	2	3	3	10	12	9	5	6	7	8	12	8
1964	70	67	61	3	4	3	3	1	2	9	10	16	2	2	1	6	10	9	5	5	6	3	2	2
1968	57	56	56	4	1	3	2	1	3	12	11	16	2	3	3	11	15	11	6	7	5	5	6	4
1972	67	61	64	4	5	4	2	4	2	7	10	9	2	4	2	5	8	9	6	5	5	7	4	5
1976	71	67	66	6	5	5	1	2	1	9	12	15	3	3	4	4	6	4	2	3	3	3	3	3
1980	67	71	62	7	5	7	0	1	2	10	7	11	4	4	5	6	4	7	3	2	3	3	2	3
1984	63	63	59	8	6	8	1	1	4	11	10	12	3	3	4	7	7	5	4	4	4	4	6	4
1988	58	55	53	13	10	13	2	4	5	7	10	11	4	4	4	6	6	4	3	2	3	8	9	5
1992	69	66	56	7	6	7	2	3	10	8	10	12	3	2	3	5	4	5	2	2	3	5	6	3
1996	62	58	46	7	7	9	2	6	10	13	13	24	6	7	3	6	6	5	1	0	3	3	2	1
2000	63	53	47	9	9	9	4	9	11	12	17	20	4	3	4	5	6	5	2	2	2	2	2	2
2004	60	49	49	10	7	6	3	4	11	11	19	16	3	4	3	7	8	10	2	3	2	6	7	3

Table 6.4 Subject area of dislikes of the Republican Party by church attendance, 1952–2004

Year	No mention			Economic			Non-economic domestic			Party philosophy			Government management			General party image			People in the party			Foreign policy		
	L	M	H	L	M	H	L	M	H	L	M	H	L	M	H	L	M	H	L	M	H	L	M	H
1952	46	57	53	30	27	29	3	2	3	5	2	3	0	0	0	8	7	7	5	4	3	2	2	1
1956	52	55	55	22	20	23	7	8	7	2	2	2	0	1	—	7	5	6	7	5	5	2	3	—
1960	55	55	53	17	20	21	6	8	6	4	3	6	2	1	1	10	4	6	2	2	3	4	7	5
1964	53	58	49	15	12	17	3	5	2	4	4	4	2	2	2	14	11	15	8	6	9	2	1	—
1968	55	57	55	14	12	15	3	3	2	6	7	7	1	0	1	12	14	12	7	6	6	2	0	—
1972	55	58	57	23	22	22	2	2	1	4	5	3	3	3	3	7	5	9	4	1	—	3	3	3
1976	51	55	57	22	21	20	2	2	—	6	7	6	2	2	2	11	7	8	4	4	4	2	2	1
1980	61	68	65	17	15	20	4	2	2	6	4	5	1	1	—	7	7	5	3	1	2	1	2	—
1984	59	62	62	18	16	18	3	5	4	9	6	5	2	2	2	3	3	4	2	—	—	4	5	3
1988	55	57	57	20	20	19	5	4	3	5	5	5	4	5	3	5	3	6	1	2	2	5	5	5
1992	48	49	52	22	25	25	7	6	3	10	7	7	3	4	5	6	6	6	2	1	2	2	2	—
1996	47	52	49	21	17	17	8	7	7	11	8	9	2	2	4	8	10	11	2	2	2	0	1	0
2000	50	48	52	18	17	20	9	8	8	11	12	6	4	3	2	7	10	10	2	1	—	0	1	—
2004	47	50	43	16	19	21	10	5	4	9	12	8	4	3	5	8	7	13	1	0	2	3	2	4

As has been the case throughout this book, the top individual positive and negative images of each party are incredibly similar among church attendance groups, and also incredibly similar to the public as a whole. All three attendance groups most commonly see the Democrats positively because they stand up for the working class and the Republicans negatively because they cater too much to big business and the wealthy. At the same time, low, moderate, and high church attenders—at least since 1964—have a top positive Republican image and top negative Democratic image that is ideological in nature.

CONCLUSION

Examining party images by different levels of church attendance has resulted in something of a mixed bag in terms of image differences. We see the, by now, familiar pattern of an increase of party images across all church attendance groups since 1980. Once again, we see that party images have become more widespread within the American electorate. We see that there is not much difference among attendance groups in terms of the presence of Democratic likes and Republican dislikes, but that there are group differences in Democratic dislikes and Republican likes, with high church attenders being more likely than low church attenders to possess such images in both cases. Looking at net party affect also clearly demonstrates that those with low levels of church attendance are more positive about the Democratic Party than are those with high levels.

In terms of image substance, there is not much differentiation between the attendance groups, with one exception. Indeed, although the usual pattern of positive images of the Democrats for economic reasons, negative images of the Democrats for party philosophy reasons, and a reversal for the Republicans are once again present here, it may well be that non-economic domestic images are the most interesting when the electorate is divided by church attendance. We now see a well-established difference in positive Republican images based on non-economic domestic issues between high and low church attenders, and we also see what is perhaps the start of such a trend in positive and negative Democratic images and negative Republican images. If cultural issues and religious salience are indeed differentiating the images of the political parties within the electorate, non-economic domestic issues would certainly be where we would expect to see these differences manifest themselves. These developments bear watching in future years.

Chapter 7

Conclusion

This examination of images held by Americans of their political parties has revealed a number of important findings. First, and perhaps most important, Americans do indeed have images of the Republican and Democratic Parties. Political parties continue to have meaning, and references to these parties generate pictures in the minds of Americans. In addition, these mental pictures have become more prevalent in recent years. Party images have risen in frequency since the 1980s, coinciding with the increase we have seen in the importance of partisanship for American politics over the same period. One could certainly make the case that the United States is more partisan today than at any point since the late nineteenth-century era of partisan torchlight parades and massive partisan rallies.[1] Recent growth in the frequency of party images likely reflects this partisan resurgence.

Americans not only have images of their political parties, they have *substantive* images of their political parties. The images held by individuals of the Democrats and the Republicans are not vacuous or ill-defined. On the contrary, asking Americans to think about the parties causes many to generate clear mental pictures related to important matters in the American polity. Americans are quite clear on how they see their two major parties, and they also see quite clearly that the parties differ from each other in important ways, as Figure 7.1 demonstrates.

When considering the electorate as a whole, economic images of the parties are the most common—at least they were until 2004. The American public sees the Democratic Party much more positively on economic issues than it does the Republican Party, another trend that has been in place throughout the entire length of this study. The Democrats' image advantage on economics arises mostly from the fact that Americans see the party as the champion of the working class and the common person in the United States, while viewing the Republicans as the party of big business and the rich. At least here, the partisan divisions of the New Deal still remain vital and meaningful.

Fortunately for the Republican Party, Americans' party images are

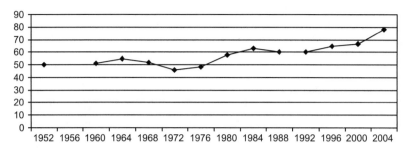

Figure 7.1 Percentage of Americans who see important differences between the parties, 1952–2004.

made up of more than economic references. As ideology has become more important in American politics, the presence of party images rooted in party philosophy has increased. In 1952 only 6 percent of Americans' party images were based on party philosophy. By 2004 the figure was at 16 percent, and the trend is moving upward. While both parties are increasingly seen in terms of party philosophy, the Republicans have benefited more from the surge in ideological and other philosophy-related party images. The GOP is more likely to be seen positively for its conservatism and opposition to big government, while the Democrats are more likely to generate a negative image because of what some Americans see as the party's excessive liberalism or tendency to engage in profligate spending. It is important to note that there are significant numbers of Americans who hold philosophical party images opposite to those described here, liking the Democrats and disliking the Republicans because of ideological or other party philosophy reasons. But these images are less common.

Party images rooted in non-economic domestic issues have also increased in recent years. As non-economic issues—such as abortion, homosexual rights, affirmative action, the environment, etc.—have assumed more prominent places on the public agenda, they have also come to make up a somewhat larger component of Americans' party images. This trend is apparent for both parties, with the Democrats tending to be seen a little more positively than the Republicans on these issues. Republicans, on the other hand, tend to be advantaged by images based on foreign policy and government management. These images are not terribly prevalent within the electorate, but they do sometimes increase in response to national or global events and, when they do, it is usually the Republicans who are seen in a more positive fashion.

Examining how party images relate to some of the most prominent cleavages in American politics also resulted in some important findings. Turning first to social class, it is clear that there are distinctions in party images held by different income groups in American society. When the likes and dislikes of both parties are considered, the Democrats have a much bigger advantage with those in the lower third of the family income distribution. Those in the lower third are much less likely to see anything they like about the Republican Party, while the reverse is true for those in the upper income third. Americans in the top third are also more likely to have a negative image of the Democratic Party. But the class differences are not as large as one might expect. There is very little difference among the income groups in terms of seeing the Democrats in a positive light, often for economic reasons. So while there are important differences in party images based on class, there are elements of similarity as well.

There are also important differences in party images present on the basis of race and ethnicity. When all partisan likes and dislikes are considered, the Democratic Party makes out much better among non-whites than it does among whites. Non-whites have somewhat higher positive and significantly lower negative images of the Democrats than do whites. Whites, on the other hand, see much more to like about the Republican Party than do non-whites. There is little difference between the races in terms of economic images—both tend to see the Democrats positively and the Republicans negatively here—but there are sizeable differences in how they see the parties in philosophical terms. Whites are much more likely to dislike the Democratic Party and like the Republican Party because of images rooted in party philosophy. Once again, we see clear differences in party images mixed with areas of similarity.

The other two electoral cleavages examined in this book—sex and religious salience—also presented both difference and similarity in terms of party images. Women and men both saw the Democratic Party positively for economic reasons. On the other hand, men are more likely than women to see the Democrats negatively based on party philosophy and are also more likely to have a favorable image of the GOP, also rooted primarily in party philosophy but increasingly, too, in economics and, in some years, foreign policy. Religious salience—measured here by church attendance—revealed perhaps the most similarity and least difference in party images of the four cleavages examined here. All church attendance levels were roughly equal in terms of having positive images of the Democrats and negative images of the Republicans. On the other hand, those Americans with high levels of attendance at worship services were more likely to hold negative Democratic and positive Republican images. In terms of substance, there was relatively little difference among attendance groups in terms of why they saw the parties in the way they did, with one exception. In the last three presidential election years, we are beginning to see differences in non-economic domestic images of the parties by level of church attendance. It will be important to see if this development continues.

IMPORTANCE OF PARTY IMAGES

We have determined that Americans do indeed have party images. These images are substantive, and they differ to a certain degree among those individuals on opposite sides of the major electoral cleavages present in contemporary American politics. But, at the end of the day, are these party images relevant to electoral outcomes? Are they important in how Americans act politically? One would assume that the answer is "yes," and in this case such an assumption would be correct. Figure 7.2 presents the Democratic presidential vote percentage for those Americans who have a positive image of the Democrats and for those with a negative image of the Republicans. Figure 7.3 shows the Republican presidential vote percentage for those having a positive GOP image and for those having a negative Democratic image. In all but two instances (negative Republican image in 1972 and negative Democratic image in 1992) those holding a certain type of image have voted for the "right" candidate. Americans

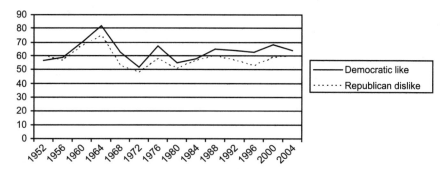

Figure 7.2 Percentage of Americans with a Democratic Party like and percentage of Americans with a Republican Party dislike voting Democratic for president, 1952–2004.

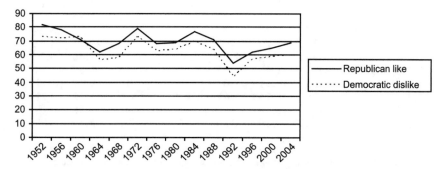

Figure 7.3 Percentage of Americans with a Republican Party like and percentage of Americans with a Democratic Party dislike voting Republican for president, 1952–2004.

with positive Democratic or negative Republican images tend to vote for Democratic presidential candidates, while those with positive Republican or negative Democratic images tend to select Republican candidates. In many instances the margins are quite large, and they have increased in recent years.

Table 7.1 presents an additional way of gauging the importance of party images. This table presents logistic regression coefficients for eight variables on the Democratic presidential vote—the possession of positive and negative images of both parties and variables representing the four electoral cleavages discussed in this book—sex, church attendance, race, and family income. A larger coefficient means a bigger effect on presidential vote. We can see that in all cases party images had a relatively large and statistically significant impact on presidential vote. Having a positive image of the Democrats or a negative image of the Republicans makes an individual more likely to vote Democratic, while having a negative Democratic image or a positive Republican image increases the chances that a person will go for a non-Democratic option on Election Day. Certainly this is not a fully specified model, but the results are impressive nonetheless.

Political parties matter in American politics, and how Americans see their parties matters as well. The American electorate has substantive images of the Republican and Democratic Parties. These images are rooted in years, and in some cases decades, of what the parties and their

Table 7.1 Logistic regression coefficients for selected variables on Democratic presidential vote, 1952–2004

Year	DL	DNL	RL	RNL	Female	Ch. Att.	White	Income
1952	**1.71**	**-1.63**	**-2.02**	**1.67**	.07	.00	**-1.48**	.14
1956	**2.31**	-.85	**-1.84**	**1.39**	.03	-.02	-.37	.02
1960	**1.89**	**-1.79**	**-1.28**	**1.46**	-.07	-.14	**-.97**	.05
1964	**1.68**	**-1.81**	**-2.05**	**1.04**	.07	-.13	**-2.81**	.01
1968	**2.34**	**-1.32**	**-1.10**	.73	.43	-.06	**-2.25**	.18
1972	**1.37**	-.69	**-1.25**	**1.08**	.39	-.34	**-1.86**	-.10
1976	**1.79**	**-1.30**	**-1.46**	.91	-.27	-.05	-.94	-.24
1980	**1.60**	**-1.21**	**-1.26**	.93	.28	-.03	**-1.75**	-.16
1984	**1.89**	-.96	**-2.34**	**1.87**	.32	-.10	**-1.46**	-.27
1988	**2.16**	-.95	**-2.42**	**1.59**	.20	-.20	**-1.37**	-.16
1992	**1.81**	**-1.05**	**-1.69**	**1.01**	.20	-.22	**-1.29**	-.12
1996	**1.97**	**-1.18**	**-1.76**	.62	.45	-.08	**-1.22**	-.22
2000	**2.67**	-.95	**-2.30**	.96	.35	-.21	-.85	-.15
2004	**1.94**	-.98	**-2.10**	**1.50**	.26	-.29	**-2.49**	-.01

Note: Significant coefficients (.05 level or better) are in bold. Presidential vote is coded 1 for Democratic and 0 otherwise, meaning that a positive coefficient means a greater likelihood of voting Democratic. All likes, dislikes, female, and white are coded as present/absent dichotomies. Family income and church attendance are used as coded in the ANES Cumulative Data File, from low to high.

leaders have said and done in the context of American politics. Robert Erikson and his colleagues argue that mass partisanship changes meaningfully in relation to how parties perform.[2] It would seem that the same is true about the party images held by Americans. Party images do reflect real differences between the parties, and they have changed over time as the parties themselves have changed. Americans use these party images to help them make sense of politics.

Voters are not alone in their use of party images: partisan leaders and officials use them as well, often to great effect. The overwhelming bulk of political information that an individual receives originates with political elites,[3] and the overwhelming bulk of these elites are partisan, often highly partisan. These partisan elites are engaged in a constant, never-ending effort to craft an electoral coalition that will enable their party to control the machinery of government.[4] A good deal of these attempts to achieve electoral success involve parties and their candidates attempting to craft appeals that some portion of the electorate will respond to favorably, and ultimately support the party's cause on Election Day.[5] Some of these appeals focus on specific issues, and policy options related to these issues. John Petrocik has clearly shown that parties tend to "own" certain issues, meaning that the electorate sees a particular party as more likely to successfully "handle" that issue than would the opposing party. Petrocik also demonstrates that parties and their candidates tend to emphasize the issues they own during campaigns, although in some instances they do try to "poach" an issue from the opposing party in an attempt to either neutralize the issue or perhaps even co-opt it as their own.[6] We can certainly see elements of this issue ownership at play in the party images we have observed throughout this book. We also know that voters tend to see political parties as collections of various social groups in society, and that they base their own partisanship at least in part on their evaluations of the parties' group collections.[7] Parties recognize this, and craft their messages accordingly. Given the large amount of group-related material we saw in the public's party images, we know these messages are received by the electorate. Once again, it is perhaps Schattschneider who sums it up best when he characterizes political parties as "salesmen of politics."[8] Parties make heavy use of party images as they attempt to close the deal with the American electorate.

We have seen that party images are crucial to voters as they attempt to make sense of American politics. They are also important to parties as they try to communicate with, and appeal to, voters. Each of these endeavors must be at least somewhat successful in order for America's representative democracy to function at an acceptable level. The "pictures in our heads" that are party images therefore play an important role in American politics.[9]

Appendix

The ANES 1948–2004 Cumulative Data File Party Likes and Dislikes Codes

For 1952–1968 the open-ended party likes and dislikes first responses are ANES Cumulative Data File variable numbers vcf0375c (Democratic likes), vcf0381c (Democratic dislikes), vcf0387c (Republican likes), and vcf0393c (Republican dislikes). For 1972–2004 the variables are vcf0375a (Democratic likes), vcf0381a (Democratic dislikes), vcf0387a (Republican likes), and vcf0393a (Republican dislikes). From 1952–1968 different codes were used for each of the four likes and dislikes. From 1972–2004 the same codes were used for all four. These codes are presented below. For the likes and dislikes that these codes represent, see *The ANES 1948–2004 Cumulative Data File* Codebook Appendix File.

1952–1968

Democratic Party Likes

People in the Party
1010–1090
General Party Images
1800–1891, 1900, 1911, 1940, 1950, 1951
Government Management
1100–1112, 1140–1190
Party Philosophy
1120, 1130, 1201, 1230–1291, 1970–1979
Economic
1210, 1220, 1300, 1340–1380, 1499, 1615–1650, 1700–1750
Non-economic Domestic
1202, 1303–1330, 1390–1392, 1400–1493, 1660–1692, 1760–1799
Foreign Policy
1500–1599

Democratic Party Dislikes

People in the Party
2010–2090
General Party Image
2800–2891, 2900, 2903, 2912, 2940, 2950, 2951, 2960
Government Management
2100–2112, 2140–2190
Party Philosophy
2120, 2121, 2130, 2201, 2230–2291, 2970–2979
Economics
2210, 2220, 2300, 2340–2380, 2499, 2615–2650, 2700–2750
Non-economic Domestic
2202, 2303–2330, 2390–2392, 2400–2493, 2660–2692, 2760–2799
Foreign Policy
2500–2599

Republican Party Likes

People in the Party
3010–3090
General Party Images
3800–3891, 3900, 3903, 3913, 3915, 3940, 3950, 3951, 3960
Government Management
3100–3112, 3149–3190
Party Philosophy
3120, 3121, 3130, 3201, 3230–3291, 3970–3879
Economics
3210, 3220, 3300, 3340–3380, 3499, 3615–3650, 3700–3750
Non-economic Domestic
3202, 3303–3330, 3390–3392, 3400–3493, 3660–3692, 3760–3799
Foreign Policy
3500–3599

Republican Party Dislikes

People in the Party
4010–4090
General Party Image
4800–4891, 4900, 4903, 4913, 4915, 4940, 4950, 4951, 4960, 4990
Government Management
4100–4112, 4140–4190
Party Philosophy
4120, 4121, 4130, 4201, 4230–4291, 4970–4979
Economics
4210, 422, 4300, 4340–4380, 4499, 4615–4650, 4700–4750

Non-economic Domestic
4202, 4303–4330, 4390–4392, 4400–4493, 4660–4692, 4760–4799
Foreign Policy
4500–4599

1972–2004

All Party Likes and Dislikes

People in the Party
0001–0097
General Party Images
0101–0132, 0135–0170, 0173–0197, 0701–0797
Government Management
0601–0604, 0607–0697
Party Philosophy
0133–0134, 0171–0172, 0605–0606, 0801–0897
Economics
0901–0907, 0811–0913, 0926–0942, 1007–1009, 1035–1037, 1046, 1201–1214, 1219–1220, 1233–1234, 1249–1250
Non-economic Domestic
0900, 0908–0910, 0914–0925, 0943–0997, 1001–1006, 1010–1033, 1038–1045, 1047–1049, 1050–1061, 1062–1070, 1215–1218, 1221–1232, 1235–1248, 1251–1297
Foreign Policy
1101–1197, 1300–1307

Notes

Preface

1. Walter Lippmann, *Public Opinion* (New York: Harcourt Brace Jovanovich, 1922).
2. Pamela Johnston Conover and Stanley Feldman, "The Role of Inference in the Perception of Political Candidates," in *Political Cognition*, ed. Richard R. Lau and David O. Sears (Hillsdale, NJ: Lawrence Erlbaum Associates, 1986), 127–158; Patrick K. Stroh, "Voters as Pragmatic Cognitive Misers: The Accuracy–Effort Trade-off in the Candidate Evaluation Process," in *Political Judgment: Structure and Process*, ed. Milton Lodge and Kathleen M. McGraw (Ann Arbor, MI: University of Michigan Press, 1995), 207–228.

I Pictures of Parties

1. E. E. Schattschneider, *Party Government* (New York: Holt, Rinehart, and Winston, 1942), 1.
2. It is now clear that the long-running assertion over approximately two decades that political parties were becoming increasingly irrelevant to American politics was simply wrong. For a few examples of work in this tradition see: David S. Broder, *The Party's Over: The Failure of Politics in America* (New York: Harper and Row, 1972); Everett Carll Ladd, Jr., *Where Have All the Voters Gone? The Fracturing of America's Political Parties* (New York: W.W. Norton, 1978); Martin P. Wattenberg, *The Decline of American Political Parties, 1952–1996* (Cambridge, MA: Harvard University Press, 1998).
3. Richard J. Trilling, *Party Image and Electoral Behavior* (New York: John Wiley and Sons, 1976).
4. For a few exceptions to this general lack of attention, see: Donald C. Baumer and Howard J. Gold, "Party Images and the American Electorate," *American Politics Quarterly* 23 (January 1995): 33–61; Thomas M. Konda and Lee Sigelman, "Public Evaluations of the American Parties, 1952–1984," *Journal of Politics* 49 (August 1987): 814–829; Arthur Sanders, "The Meaning of Party Images," *Western Political Quarterly* 41 (September 1988): 583–599.
5. V.O. Key, Jr., *Public Opinion and American Democracy* (New York: Alfred A. Knopf, 1961); Donald R. Matthews and James W. Prothro, "Southern Images of Political Parties: An Analysis of White and Negro Attitudes," *Journal of Politics* 26 (February 1964): 82–111; Gerald M. Pomper, *Voters' Choice: Varieties of American Electoral Behavior* (New York: Dodd, Mead, and Company, 1975); Trilling, *Party Image and Electoral Behavior*.

6. Trilling, *Party Image and Electoral Behavior*.
7. Edward G. Carmines, Steven H. Renten, and James A. Stimson, "Events and Alignments: The Party Image Link," in *Controversies in Voting Behavior*, 2nd ed., ed. Richard G. Niemi and Herbert F. Weisberg (Washington, DC: CQ Press, 1984), 545–560.
8. Baumer and Gold, "Party Images and the American Electorate"; Key, *Public Opinion and American Democracy*; William G. Jacoby, "The Impact of Party Identification on Issue Attitudes," *American Journal of Political Science* 32 (August 1988): 643–661.
9. Charles Sellers, "The Equilibrium Cycle in Two-party Politics," *Public Opinion Quarterly* 29 (spring 1965): 16–38.
10. Bernard R. Berelson, Paul F. Lazarsfeld, and William N. McPhee, *Voting: A Study of Opinion Formation in a Presidential Campaign* (Chicago: University of Chicago Press, 1954); Paul F. Lazarsfeld, Bernard Berelson, and Hazel Gaudet, *The People's Choice: How the Voter Makes Up His Mind in a Presidential Campaign*, 2nd ed. (New York: Columbia University Press, 1948). The quotation is from p. 27 of *The People's Choice*.
11. Angus Campbell et al., *The American Voter* (New York: John Wiley and Sons, 1960).
12. Norman H. Nie, Sidney Verba, and John R. Petrocik, *The Changing American Voter* (Cambridge, MA: Harvard University Press, 1976). See also Gerald M. Pomper, "Toward a More Responsible Two-party System? What, Again?" *Journal of Politics* 33 (November 1971): 916–940; Gerald M. Pomper, "From Confusion to Clarity: Issues and American Voters, 1956–1968," *American Political Science Review* 66 (June 1972): 415–428.
13. Morris P. Fiorina, *Retrospective Voting in American National Elections* (New Haven, CT: Yale University Press, 1981); V.O. Key, Jr., with the assistance of Milton C. Cummings, Jr., *The Responsible Electorate: Rationality in Presidential Voting, 1936–1960* (Cambridge, MA: Harvard University Press, 1966).
14. The most recent work that presents anything more than a cursory analysis of party images in the United States is Baumer and Gold, "Party Images and the American Electorate," referenced above.
15. Jon R. Bond and Richard Fleisher, eds., *Polarized Politics: Congress and the President in a Partisan Era* (Washington, DC: CQ Press, 2000); Tim Groseclose, Steve D. Levitt, and James M. Snyder, "Comparing Interest Group Scores Across Time and Chambers: Adjusted ADA Scores for the U.S. Congress," *American Political Science Review* 93 (March 1999): 33–50; Gary C. Jacobson, "The Electoral Basis of Polarization in Congress" (paper presented at the Annual Meeting of the American Political Science Association, Washington, DC, 2000); Keith T. Poole and Howard Rosenthal, "The Polarization of American Politics," *Journal of Politics* 46 (November 1984): 1061–1079; Keith T. Poole and Howard Rosenthal, "Patterns of Congressional Voting," *American Journal of Political Science* 35 (February 1991): 228–278; Keith T. Poole and Howard Rosenthal, *Congress: A Political–Economic History of Roll Call Voting* (New York: Oxford University Press, 1997); David W. Rohde, *Parties and Leaders in the Postreform House* (Chicago: University of Chicago Press, 1991); Barbara Sinclair, "The Dream Fulfilled? Party Development in Congress, 1950–2000," in *Responsible Partisanship? The Evolution of American Parties Since 1950*, ed. John C. Green and Paul S. Herrnson (Lawrence, KS: University Press of Kansas, 2002), 121–140; Jeffrey M. Stonecash, Mark D. Brewer, and Mack D. Mariani, *Diverging Parties: Social Change, Realignment, and Party Polarization* (Boulder, CO: Westview Press, 2003); Andrew J. Taylor, "The Ideological

Development of the Parties in Washington, 1947–1994," *Polity* 29 (winter 1996): 273–292.

16. Mark D. Brewer and Jeffrey M. Stonecash, *Split: Class and Cultural Divides in American Politics* (Washington, DC: CQ Press, 2007); Barbara Sinclair, *Party Wars: Polarization and the Politics of National Policy Making* (Norman, OK: University of Oklahoma Press, 2006).

17. Daryl J. Levinson and Richard H. Pildes, "Separation of Parties, Not Powers," *Harvard Law Review* 119 (June 2006): 2312–2386.

18. John H. Aldrich, "Political Parties in a Critical Era," *American Politics Quarterly* 27 (January 1999): 9–32; Larry M. Bartels, "Electoral Continuity and Change, 1868–1996," *Electoral Studies* 17 (September 1998): 301–326; Larry M. Bartels, "Partisanship and Voting Behavior, 1952–1996," *American Journal of Political Science* 44 (January 2000): 35–50; Marc J. Hetherington, "Resurgent Mass Partisanship: The Role of Elite Polarization," *American Political Science Review* 95 (September 2001): 619–631; Jeffrey M. Stonecash, *Political Parties Matter: Realignment and the Return of Partisan Voting* (Boulder, CO: Lynne Rienner, 2006).

19. Sharon E. Jarvis, *The Talk of the Party: Political Labels, Symbolic Capital, and American Life* (Lanham, MD: Rowman and Littlefield, 2005).

20. David C. Kimball, "Priming Partisan Evaluations of Congress," *Legislative Studies Quarterly* 30 (February 2005): 63–84.

21. For an expanded discussion of this point, see John Aldrich, "Electoral Democracy during Politics as Usual—and Unusual," in *Electoral Democracy*, ed. Michael B. MacKuen and George Rabinowitz (Ann Arbor, MI: University of Michigan Press, 2003): 270–310. For perhaps the classic statement of the elite-driven, top-down model, see John R. Zaller, *The Nature and Origins of Mass Opinion* (New York: Cambridge University Press, 1992).

22. For some works that examine the issue of political polarization in the United States, see Alan Abramowitz and Kyle Saunders, "Why Can't We All Just Get Along? The Reality of a Polarized America," *The Forum* 3 (2005); Brewer and Stonecash, *Split*; Morris P. Fiorina, with Samuel J. Abrams and Jeremy C. Pope, *Culture War? The Myth of a Polarized America* (New York: Pearson/Longman, 2006); Thomas Frank, *What's the Matter with Kansas: How Conservatives Won the Heart of America* (New York: Henry Holt and Company, 2004); Gary C. Jacobson, *A Divider, Not a Uniter: George W. Bush and the American People* (New York: Pearson/Longman, 2007).

23. Gary C. Jacobson, "A House and Senate Divided: The Clinton Legacy and the Congressional Elections of 2000," *Political Science Quarterly* 116 (spring 2001): 5–27; John McAdams, "The Dynamics of Voter Attitudes: Reevaluating the Role of Partisanship" (paper presented at the Annual Meeting of the American Political Science Association, Boston, MA, 2002); Warren E. Miller and J. Merrill Shanks, *The New American Voter* (Cambridge, MA: Harvard University Press, 1996); Gerald M. Pomper and Marc D. Weiner, "Toward a More Responsible Two-party Voter: The Evolving Bases of Partisanship," in *Responsible Partisanship? The Evolution of American Parties Since 1950*, ed. John C. Green and Paul S. Herrnson (Lawrence, KS: University Press of Kansas), 181–200.

24. Alan I. Abramowitz and Kyle L. Saunders, "Ideological Realignment in the U.S. Electorate," *Journal of Politics* 60 (August 1998): 634–652; Jeffrey Levine, Edward G. Carmines, and Robert Huckfeldt, "The Rise of Ideology in the Post-New Deal Party System, 1972–1992," *American Politics Quarterly* 25 (January 1997): 19–34; Michael B. MacKuen et al., "Elections and the

Dynamics of Ideological Representation," in *Electoral Democracy*, ed. Michael B. MacKuen and George Rabinowitz, 200–237; Gerald M. Pomper, "The 2000 Presidential Election: Why Gore Lost," *Political Science Quarterly* 116 (summer 2001): 201–233; Kyle L. Saunders and Alan I. Abramowitz, "Ideological Realignment and Active Partisans in the American Electorate," *American Politics Research* 32 (May 2004): 285–309; William D. Schreckhise and Todd G. Shields, "Ideological Realignment in the Contemporary U.S. Electorate Revisited," *Social Science Quarterly* 84 (September 2003): 596–612.

25. For change at the elite level, see: Edward G. Carmines and James A. Stimson, *Issue Evolution: Race and the Transformation of American Politics* (Princeton, NJ: Princeton University Press, 1989); Geoffrey C. Layman, " 'Culture Wars' in the American Party System: Religious and Cultural Change among Partisan Activists Since 1972," *American Politics Quarterly* 27 (January 1999): 89–121; Geoffrey C. Layman, *The Great Divide: Religious and Cultural Conflict in American Party Politics* (New York: Columbia University Press, 2001); Kara Lindaman and Donald P. Haider-Markel, "Issue Evolution, Political Parties, and the Culture Wars," *Political Research Quarterly* 55 (March 2002): 91–110; Nicol C. Rae, "Class and Culture: American Political Cleavages in the Twentieth Century," *Western Political Quarterly* 45 (September 1992): 629–650. For changes at the mass level, see: Mark D. Brewer, "The Rise of Partisanship and the Expansion of Partisan Conflict within the American Electorate," *Political Research Quarterly* 58 (June 2005): 219–229; Edward G. Carmines and Geoffrey C. Layman, "Issue Evolution in Postwar American Politics: Old Certainties and Fresh Tensions," in *Present Discontents: American Politics in the Very Late Twentieth Century*, ed. Byron E. Shafer (Chatham, NJ: Chatham House Publishers, 1997), 89–134; Geoffrey C. Layman and Thomas M. Carsey, "Party Polarization and Party Structuring of Policy Attitudes: A Comparison of Three NES Panel Studies," *Political Behavior* 24 (September 2002): 199–236; Geoffrey C. Layman and Thomas M. Carsey, "Party Polarization and 'Conflict Extension' in the American Electorate," *American Journal of Political Science* 46 (October 2002): 786–802.

26. Henry E. Brady and Paul M. Sniderman, "Attitude Attribution: A Group Basis for Political Reasoning," *American Political Science Review* 79 (December 1985): 1061–1078; Paul M. Sniderman, Richard A. Brody, and Philip E. Tetlock. *Reasoning and Choice: Exploration in Political Psychology* (New York: Cambridge University Press, 1991).

27. Samuel L. Popkin, *The Reasoning Voter: Communication and Persuasion in Presidential Campaigns* (Chicago: University of Chicago Press, 1991).

28. Vincent L. Hutchings, *Public Opinion and Democratic Accountability: How Citizens Learn about Politics* (Princeton, NJ: Princeton University Press, 2003).

29. Pamela Johnston Conover and Stanley Feldman, "The Role of Inference in the Perception of Political Candidates," in *Political Cognition*, ed. Richard R. Lau and David O. Sears (Hillsdale, NJ: Lawrence Erlbaum Associates, 1986), 127–158; Pamela Johnston Conover and Stanley Feldman, "Candidate Perception in an Ambiguous World: Campaigns, Cues, and Inference Processes," *American Journal of Political Science* 33 (November 1989): 912–940.

30. Wendy M. Rahn, "The Role of Partisan Stereotypes in Information Processing about Political Candidates," *American Journal of Political Science* 37 (May 1993): 472–496.

2 Party Images in the Electorate as a Whole

1. Samuel L. Popkin, *The Reasoning Voter: Communication and Persuasion in Presidential Campaigns* (Chicago: University of Chicago Press, 1991).
2. Donald C. Baumer and Howard J. Gold, "Party Images and the American Electorate," *American Politics Quarterly* 23 (January 1995): 33–61; Angus Campbell et al., *The American Voter* (New York: John Wiley and Sons, 1960), chap. 3; Thomas M. Konda and Lee Sigelman, "Public Evaluations of the American Parties, 1952–1984," *Journal of Politics* 49 (August 1987): 814–829; Donald R. Matthews and James W. Prothro, "Southern Images of Political Parties: An Analysis of White and Negro Attitudes," *Journal of Politics* 26 (February 1964): 82–111; Arthur Sanders, "The Meaning of Party Images," *Western Political Quarterly* 41 (September 1988): 583–599; Richard J. Trilling, *Party Image and Electoral Behavior* (New York: John Wiley and Sons, 1976).
3. Trilling, *Party Image and Electoral Behavior*, p. 62.
4. This is true for all years except 1972, when the maximum number of likes and dislikes recorded per party was three.
5. Steven C. Craig, "The Decline of Partisanship in the United States: A Re-examination of the Neutrality Hypothesis," *Political Behavior* 7 (March 1985): 57–78; John E. Stanga and James F. Sheffield, "The Myth of Zero Partisanship: Attitudes toward American Political Parties, 1964–1984," *American Journal of Political Science* 31 (November 1987): 829–855.
6. John G. Geer, "Critical Realignments and the Public Opinion Poll," *Journal of Politics* 53 (May 1991): 434–453; John G. Geer, "The Electorate's Partisan Evaluations: Evidence of a Continuing Democratic Edge," *Public Opinion Quarterly* 55 (summer 1991): 218–231; Martin P. Wattenberg, "The Hollow Realignment: Partisan Change in a Candidate-centered Era," *Public Opinion Quarterly* 51 (spring 1987): 58–74.
7. John G. Geer, "What Do Open-ended Questions Measure?" *Public Opinion Quarterly* 52 (autumn 1988): 365–371.
8. David G. Lawrence, "The Collapse of the Democratic Majority: Economics and Vote Choice since 1952," *Western Political Quarterly* (December 1991): 797–820.
9. The American National Election Studies, *The 1948–2004 ANES Cumulative Data File* [dataset], Stanford University and University of Michigan [producers and distributors], 2005.
10. Education levels are created from the *1948–2004 ANES Cumulative Data File* variable vcf0140a. "Some College" includes AA degrees.
11. There is evidence that education might have less of such an impact among African Americans. See James M. Glaser, "Black and White Perceptions of Party Differences," *Political Behavior* 17 (June 1995): 155–177.
12. This represents a continuation of the pattern found by Trilling over thirty years ago. Trilling, *Party Image and Electoral Behavior*.
13. This is not to claim that there is nothing of value in likes/dislikes 2–5. Indeed, multiple mentions can indicate a more developed image of the parties, and indeed we see that the numbers of likes and dislikes increase with education. However, research in psychology indicates that first responses are indeed the most salient, and I am most interested here in the most salient images that Americans have of their parties. Open-ended questions tap into salient information, and the first response to such questions should produce the most salient information. See John G. Geer, "Do Open-ended Questions Measure 'Salient' Issues?" *Public Opinion Quarterly* 55 (autumn 1991): 360–370; Stanley Kelley, *Interpreting Elections* (Princeton, NJ: Princeton University Press, 1983);

David E. RePass, "Issue Salience and Party Choice," *American Political Science Review* 65 (June 1971): 389–400; Shelley E. Taylor and Susan T. Fiske, "Salience, Attention, and Attribution: Top of the Head Phenomena," in *Advances in Experimental Social Psychology*, ed. Leonard Berkowitz (New York: Academic Press, 1978), 250–288. In addition, there seems to be little difference in terms of how multiple party image holders and non-multiple party image holders behave electorally. Certainly the likelihood of an individual voting Democratic or Republican increases as the number of Democratic or Republican likes increases, and the likelihood of voting Democratic or Republican decreases as the number of Democratic or Republican dislikes increases. But comparing those who do not have a multiple image of the parties (no more than one like or dislike of either the Democrats or the Republicans) with those who do have at least one multiple image (at least one instance with more than one like or dislike of the Democrats or the Republicans) produces very little difference. Table 2.5 presents this comparison for presidential vote from 1952–2004.

14. The categorization scheme utilized here is somewhat different from the scheme contained in the NES data, but is relatively self-explanatory and straightforward. The "people in the party" category is made up of individuals in the party (e.g., Bill Clinton or George W. Bush), along with responses such as "They have good leaders" and "I don't like their ticket." The "general party image" category contains responses such as "I've always been a Republican" or "I just don't like them." "Government management" is also straightforward, consisting of responses referring to efficiency, corruption, taking care of problems (non-specific), etc. The "party philosophy" category is made up of ideological references (e.g., too liberal, or not conservative enough), references to the parties' views on government, and other responses that speak somehow to what the respondent thinks the party stands for and/or believes in, such as a party being for equality, or compassionate, or socialistic. The "economic" category consists of any response mentioning a type of economic group (e.g., "They are for the common man" or "They help business") as well as specific economic policy mentions such as references to taxes or unemployment

Table 2.5 Percentage of Democratic presidential vote for non-multiple party image holders and multiple party image holders, 1952–2004

Year	Non-multiple image holders	Multiple image holders
1952	40	42
1956	32	44
1960	43	52
1964	73	64
1968	40	41
1972	34	37
1976	47	51
1980	37	42
1984	35	46
1988	46	47
1992	44	50
1996	51	49
2000	49	52
2004	46	50

policy. "Non-economic domestic" consists of almost all domestic policy mentions such as agriculture, civil rights, abortion, veterans affairs, etc. The "foreign policy" category contains all references to relations with other nations, mentions of a general policy stance (e.g., isolationist) or for a strong military, mentions of a specific policy, such as SALT II, and all mentions related to military spending. The vast majority of likes and dislikes fit quite cleanly into one category or another and the few that do not are mentioned by so few people as to be irrelevant with one significant exception. A number of respondents give likes and dislikes that the NES places in a response labeled "For government activity, believe government should take care of things, for big government, supports social programs and spending." A similar response exists for those opposed to such things. (This is the current wording, in place since 1972. The wording—but not the substance—is somewhat different from 1952–1968.) After much consideration (and waffling as well) I decided to place these responses in the "party philosophy" category. Of course, a case can be made that these responses could also fit into the "economic" category. There are a relatively large number of these responses, especially in recent years, so moving them into the "economic" category would obviously change the results presented here. The full categorization scheme is presented in the Appendix.

15. The negative foreign policy image of the Democrats in these years is not surprising given that in both years a Democratic president with the backing of a Democratic Congress was conducting an unpopular war.

16. Baumer and Gold assign a good deal of the causality of these increases to Ronald Reagan's two terms as president. They argue that Reagan's conservative ideology and style of governance clarified the differences between the parties to voters, and made partisan cues more salient. It is quite likely that Baumer and Gold are correct in this assertion. Baumer and Gold, "Party Images and the American Electorate"; Donald C. Baumer and Howard J. Gold, "Party Images After the Clinton Years" (paper presented at the Annual Meeting of the New England Political Science Association, Portland, ME, 2002).

17. Baumer and Gold, "Party Images and the American Electorate"; Donald Green, Bradley Palmquist, and Eric Schickler, *Partisan Hearts and Minds: Political Parties and the Social Identities of Voters* (New Haven, CT: Yale University Press, 2002); V.O. Key, Jr., *Public Opinion and American Democracy* (New York: Alfred A. Knopf, 1961); Sanders, "The Meaning of Party Images"; Trilling, *Party Image and Electoral Behavior*.

3 Party Images and the Class Cleavage

1. Alexis de Tocqueville, *Democracy in America*, 2 vols., ed. Phillips Bradley, introduction by Daniel J. Boorstin (New York: Vintage Books, 1990). Another famous European observer, James Bryce, acknowledged that there were different classes in American society, but that these differences were politically irrelevant. James Bryce, *The American Commonwealth*, 2 vols. (New York: G.P. Putnam and Sons, 1959). For an important discussion of the importance of classlessness for American political development, see Louis Hartz, *The Liberal Tradition in America* (New York: Harcourt, Brace, and World, 1955).

2. V.O. Key, Jr., *Southern Politics in State and Nation*, new edition (Knoxville, TN: University of Tennessee Press, 1984), 307.

3. Lawrence Goodwyn, *Democratic Promise: The Populist Moment in America* (New York: Oxford University Press, 1976); Samuel P. Hays, "The Politics of Reform in Municipal Government in the Progressive Era," *Pacific Northwest*

Quarterly 55 (October 1964): 157–169; John D. Hicks, *The Populist Revolt* (Minneapolis, MN: University of Minnesota Press, 1931); Dennis R. Judd and Todd Swanstrom, *City Politics: The Political Economy of Urban America*, 6th ed. (New York: Pearson/Longman, 2008); Robert H. Wiebe, *The Search for Order, 1877–1920* (New York: Hill and Wang, 1967).

4. Everett Carll Ladd, Jr., with Charles D. Hadley, *Transformations of the American Party System: Political Coalitions from the New Deal to the 1970s* (New York: W.W. Norton, 1975): William E. Leuchtenburg, *Franklin D. Roosevelt and the New Deal, 1932–1940* (New York: Harper and Row, 1963); David Plotke, *Building a Democratic Political Order: Reshaping American Liberalism in the 1930s and 1940s* (New York: Cambridge University Press, 1996); Arthur Schlesinger, Jr., *The Politics of Upheaval* (Boston: Houghton Mifflin, 1960).

5. Edward G. Carmines and James A. Stimson, *Issue Exploitation: Race and the Transformation of American Politics* (Princeton, NJ: Princeton University Press, 1989); William E. Leuchtenburg, *The White House Looks South: Franklin D. Roosevelt, Harry S. Truman, and Lyndon B. Johnson* (Baton Rouge, LA: Louisiana State University Press, 2005).

6. Kevin P. Phillips, *The Emerging Republican Majority* (New Rochelle, NY: Arlington House, 1969). Democratic strategists Richard Scammon and Ben Wattenberg feared that Phillips was correct. Richard M. Scammon and Ben J. Wattenberg, *The Real Majority* (New York: Conrad-McCann, 1970).

7. For just a few of the many examples of such work, see: Ladd with Hadley, *Transformations of the American Party System*; David G. Lawrence, "The Collapse of the Democratic Majority: Economics and Vote Choice Since 1952," *Western Political Quarterly* 44 (December 1991): 797–820; David G. Lawrence, *The Collapse of the Democratic Presidential Majority* (Boulder, CO: Westview Press, 1996); Harold W. Stanley and Richard G. Niemi, "Partisanship and Group Support, 1952–1988," *American Politics Quarterly* 19 (April 1991): 189–210; Harold W. Stanley and Richard G. Niemi, "Party Coalitions in Transition: Partisanship and Group Support, 1952–1996," in *Controversies in Voting Behavior*, 4th ed., ed. Richard G. Niemi and Herbert F. Weisberg (Washington, DC: CQ Press, 2001), 387–404.

8. Robert Huckfeldt and Carol Weitzel Kohfeld, *Race and the Decline of Class in American Politics* (Urbana, IL: University of Illinois Press, 1989).

9. Thomas Byrne Edsall with Mary D. Edsall, *Chain Reaction: The Impact of Race, Rights, and Taxes on American Politics* (New York: W.W. Norton, 1991).

10. Kenneth S. Baer, *Reinventing Democrats: The Politics of Liberalism from Reagan to Clinton* (Lawrence, KS: University Press of Kansas, 2000).

11. Ronald Inglehart, *The Silent Revolution: Changing Values and Political Styles Among Western Publics* (Princeton, NJ: Princeton University Press, 1977); Ronald Inglehart, "Post-materialism in an Environment of Insecurity," *American Political Science Review* 75 (December 1981): 880–900; Ronald Inglehart, *Culture Shift in Advanced Industrial Society* (Princeton, NJ: Princeton University Press, 1990); Ronald Inglehart, *Modernization and Postmodernization: Cultural, Economic, and Political Change in 43 Societies* (Princeton, NJ: Princeton University Press, 1997).

12. Nicol C. Rae, "Class and Culture: American Political Cleavages in the Twentieth Century," *Western Political Quarterly* 45 (September 1992): 629–650.

13. Larry M. Bartels, "What's the Matter with *What's the Matter with Kansas?*" *Quarterly Journal of Political Science* 1 (March 2006): 201–226; Robert S. Erikson, Thomas D. Lancaster, and David W. Romero, "Group Components of the Presidential Vote, 1952–1984," *Journal of Politics* 51 (May 1989): 337–346;

Jeffrey M. Stonecash, *Class and Party in American Politics* (Boulder, CO: Westview Press, 2000); Jeffrey M. Stonecash et al., "Class and Party: Secular Realignment and the Survival of Democrats Outside of the South," *Political Research Quarterly* 53 (December 2000): 731–752.

14. Jonathan Knuckey, "Explaining Recent Changes in the Partisan Identifications of Southern Whites," *Political Research Quarterly* 59 (March 2006): 57–70; Richard Nadeau, Richard G. Niemi, Harold W. Stanley, and Jean-Francois Godbout, "Class, Party, and South/Non-South Differences: An Update," *American Politics Research* 32 (January 2004): 52–67; Richard Nadeau and Harold W. Stanley, "Class Polarization in Partisanship among Native Southern Whites, 1952–1990," *American Journal of Political Science* 37 (August 1993): 900–919; Byron E. Shafer and Richard Johnston, *The End of Southern Exceptionalism: Class, Race, and Partisan Change in the Postwar South* (Cambridge, MA: Harvard University Press, 2006); Martin P. Wattenberg, "The Building of a Republican Regional Base in the South: The Elephant Crosses the Mason–Dixon Line," *Public Opinion Quarterly* 55 (autumn 1991): 424–431.

15. Richard F. Hamilton, *Class and Politics in the United States* (New York: John Wiley and Sons, 1972).

16. Sheldon Danziger and Peter Gottschalk, *America Unequal* (Cambridge, MA: Harvard University Press, 1995); Edward L. Glaeser, "Inequality," *National Bureau of Economic Research Working Paper No. 11511* (Cambridge, MA, June 2005).

17. Jared Bernstein, Elizabeth McNichol, and Karen Lyons, "Pulling Apart: A State-by-state Analysis of Income Trends," Center on Budget and Policy Priorities and Economic Policy Institute, Washington, DC, January 2006; Mark D. Brewer and Jeffrey M. Stonecash, *Split: Class and Cultural Divides in American Politics* (Washington, DC: CQ Press, 2007).

18. Jo Freeman, "The Political Culture of the Democratic and Republican Parties," *Political Science Quarterly* 101 (1986): 327–356; John Gerring, *Party Ideologies in America, 1828–1996* (New York: Cambridge University Press, 1998).

19. Brewer and Stonecash, *Split*; James W. Ceaser, "The Theory of Governance of the Reagan Administration," in *The Reagan Presidency and the Governing of America*, ed. Lester M. Salamon and Michael S. Lund (Washington, DC: Urban Institute Press, 1984), 57–87; John Micklethwait and Adrian Wooldridge, *The Right Nation: Conservative Power in America* (New York: Penguin Press, 2004).

20. In the words of Mary and Robert Jackman, "Organized political life [in the US] provides the electorate with only a sparse education in class issues." Mary R. Jackman and Robert W. Jackman, *Class Awareness in the United States* (Berkeley, CA: University of California Press, 1983), 215.

21. William G. Mayer, *The Changing American Mind: How and Why American Public Opinion Changed between 1960 and 1988* (Ann Arbor, MI: University of Michigan Press, 1992), p. 75.

22. The ANES Cumulative Data File presents family income (vcf0114) in five groups: 0–16 percentile, 17–33 percentile, 34–67 percentile, 68–95 percentile, and 96–100 percentile. In this analysis, the first two groups are combined to create the lower income third (0–33 percentile), the third group is the middle income third (34–67 percentile), and the last two groups are combined to create the top income third (68–100 percentile).

23. For a more in-depth discussion of the differing ways to measure class and the status of family income as the most preferable option, see Stonecash, *Class and Party in American Politics*.

24. In 1968 the top Democratic dislike among those in the lower third of the family income distribution was the party's actions related to the Vietnam War; in 1988 it was that the party was poorly organized, and in both 2000 and 2004 it was that the Democrats could not be trusted.

4 Party Images and Race and Ethnicity

1. Gunnar Myrdal, *An American Dilemma: The Negro Problem and Modern Democracy* (New York: Harper and Brothers, 1944), xlvii.
2. Martin Luther King, Jr., "I've Been to the Mountaintop" (Memphis, TN, April 3, 1968).
3. For the original statement on symbolic racism, see David O. Sears and Donald R. Kinder, "Racial Tension and Voting in Los Angeles," in *Los Angeles: Viability and Prospects for Metropolitan Leadership*, ed. Werner Z. Hirsch (New York: Praeger, 1971), 51–88. For further explications over the years (this list is not exhaustive), see Donald R. Kinder and Tali Mendelberg, "Individualism Reconsidered: Principles and Prejudice in Contemporary American Opinion," in *Racialized Politics: The Debate about Racism in America*, ed. David O. Sears, Jim Sidanius, and Lawrence Bobo (Chicago: University of Chicago Press, 2000), 44–74; Donald R. Kinder and David O. Sears, "Prejudice and Politics: Symbolic Racism Versus Racial Threats to the Good Life," *Journal of Personality and Social Psychology* 40 (March 1981): 414–431; Donald R. Kinder and Nicholas Winter, "Exploring the Racial Divide: Blacks, Whites, and Opinion on National Policy," *American Journal of Political Science* 45 (April 2001): 439–456; David O. Sears, "Symbolic Racism," in *Eliminating Racism: Profiles in Controversy*, ed. Phyllis A. Katz and Dalmas A. Taylor (New York: Plenum Press, 1988), 53–84; David O. Sears and P.J. Henry, "The Origins of Symbolic Racism," *Journal of Personality and Social Psychology* 85 (August 2003): 259–275; David O. Sears, P.J. Henry, and Rick Kosterman, "Egalitarian Values and Contemporary Racial Politics," in *Racialized Politics*, ed. Sears, Sidanius, and Bobo, 75–117; Christopher Tarman and David O. Sears, "The Conceptualization and Measurement of Symbolic Racism," *Journal of Politics* 67 (August 2005): 731–761.
4. Donald R. Kinder and Lynn M. Sanders, *Divided by Color: Racial Politics and Democratic Ideals* (Chicago: University of Chicago Press, 1996).
5. Paul M. Sniderman and Thomas Piazza, *The Scar of Race* (Cambridge, MA: The Belknap Press of Harvard University Press, 1993). See also Jon Hurwitz and Mark Peffley, "Introduction," in *Perception and Prejudice: Race and Politics in the United States*, ed. Jon Hurwitz and Mark Peffley (New Haven, CT: Yale University Press, 1998), 1–16; Paul M. Sniderman and Edward G. Carmines, *Reaching Beyond Race* (Cambridge, MA: Harvard University Press, 1997); Paul M. Sniderman, Gretchen Crosby, and William G. Howell, "The Politics of Race," in *Racialized Politics*, ed. Sears, Sidanius, and Bobo, 236–279. For a comparison of symbolic racism and rival explanations for differences in opinion on racial policy, see R. Michael Alvarez and John Brehm, "Are Americans Ambivalent Towards Racial Policies?" *American Journal of Political Science* 41 (April 1997): 345–374.
6. Lawrence Bobo, "Group Conflict, Prejudice, and the Paradox of Contemporary Racial Attitudes," in *Eliminating Racism*, ed. Katz and Taylor, 85–114; Lawrence Bobo and James R. Klugel, "Opposition to Race Targeting: Self Interest, Stratification Ideology, or Racial Attitudes?" *American Sociological Review* 58 (August 1993): 443–464. See also Michael Hughes, "Symbolic

Racism, Old-fashioned Racism, and Whites' Opposition to Affirmative Action," in *Racial Attitudes in the 1990s: Continuity and Change*, ed. Steven A. Tuch and Jack K. Martin (Westport, CT: Praeger, 1997), 46–75.

7. Mary R. Jackman, *The Velvet Glove: Paternalism and Conflict in Gender, Class, and Race Relations* (Berkeley, CA: University of California Press, 1994). See also Jim Sidanius et al., "It's Not Affirmative Action, It's the Blacks: The Continuing Relevance of Race in American Politics," in *Racialized Politics*, ed. Sears, Sidanius, and Bobo, 191–235.

8. Charlotte Steeh, review of *The Scar of Race*, by Paul M. Sniderman and Thomas Piazza, *Public Opinion Quarterly* 59 (summer 1995): 316–319. For what is perhaps the most balanced examination of these competing views of the relevance of race, see Howard Schuman et al., *Racial Attitudes in America: Trends and Interpretations*, rev. ed. (Cambridge, MA: Harvard University Press, 1997).

9. Kinder and Sanders, *Divided by Color*; Kinder and Winter, "Exploring the Racial Divide: Blacks, Whites, and Opinion on National Policy"; David O. Sears et al., "Race in American Politics: Framing the Debate," in *Racialized Politics*, ed. Sears, Sidanius, and Bobo, 1–43; Steven A. Tuch, Lee Sigelman, and Jack K. Martin, "Fifty Years after Myrdal: Blacks' Policy Attitudes in the 1990s," in *Racial Attitudes in the 1990s*, ed. Tuch and Martin, 226–237.

10. Lucius J. Barker and Mack H. Jones, *African Americans and the American Political System*, 3rd ed. (Englewood Cliffs, NJ: Prentice Hall, 1994); Kinder and Sanders, *Divided by Color*; Tali Mendelberg, *The Race Card: Campaign Strategy, Implicit Messages, and the Norm of Inequality* (Princeton, NJ: Princeton University Press, 2001); Schuman et al., *Racial Attitudes in America*; Lee Sigelman and Susan Welch, *Black Americans' Views of Racial Inequality: The Dream Deferred* (New York: Cambridge University Press, 1991);

11. Martin Gilens, "Racial Attitudes and Race-neutral Social Policies: White Opposition to Welfare and the Politics of Racial Inequality," in *Perception and Prejudice*, ed. Hurwitz and Peffley, 171–201; Martin Gilens, *Why Americans Hate Welfare: Race, Media, and the Politics of Anti-poverty Policy* (Chicago: University of Chicago Press, 1999); Mendelberg, *The Race Card*; William Julius Wilson, *When Work Disappears: The World of the New Urban Poor* (New York: Random House, 1996).

12. Edward G. Carmines and James A. Stimson, *Issue Evolution: Race and the Transformation of American Politics* (Princeton, NJ: Princeton University Press, 1989); Michael K. Fauntroy, *Republicans and the Black Vote* (Boulder, CO: Lynne Rienner, 2007); William E. Leuchtenburg, *The White House Looks South: Franklin D. Roosevelt, Harry S. Truman, and Lyndon B. Johnson* (Baton Rouge, LA: Louisiana State University Press, 2005); Samuel Lubell, *The Future of American Politics*, 2nd ed., rev. (Garden City, NY: Doubleday Anchor Books, 1956).

13. Thomas Byrne Edsall, with Mary D. Edsall, *Chain Reaction: The Impact of Race, Rights, and Taxes on American Politics* (New York: W.W. Norton, 1991); Robert Huckfeldt and Carol Weitzel Kohfeld, *Race and the Decline of Class in American Politics* (Urbana, IL: University of Illinois Press, 1989); Kinder and Sanders, *Divided by Color*; Jeremy D. Mayer, *Running on Race: Racial Politics in Presidential Campaigns, 1960–2000* (New York: Random House, 2002); Katherine Tate, *From Protest to Politics: The New Black Voters in American Elections* (New York and Cambridge, MA: Russell Sage Foundation and Harvard University Press, 1993); Aaron Wildavsky, "The Goldwater Phenomenon: Purists, Politicians, and the Two-party System," *Review of Politics* 27 (July 1965): 386–413.

14. Nicol C. Rae, *The Decline and Fall of the Liberal Republicans from 1952 to the Present* (New York: Oxford University Press, 1989); David W. Rohde, *Parties and Leaders in the Postreform House* (Chicago: University of Chicago Press, 1991); Jeffrey M. Stonecash, Mark D. Brewer, and Mack D. Mariani, *Diverging Parties: Social Change, Realignment, and Party Polarization* (Boulder, CO: Westview Press, 2003).

15. Michael C. Dawson, *Behind the Mule: Race and Class in African American Politics* (Princeton, NJ: Princeton University Press, 1994); Tate, *From Protest to Politics*.

16. Kathleen Hall Jamieson, *Dirty Politics: Deception, Distraction, and Democracy* (New York: Oxford University Press, 1992); Mendelberg, *The Race Card*.

17. Dan T. Carter, *From George Wallace to Newt Gingrich: Race in the Conservative Counterrevolution* (Baton Rouge, LA: Louisiana State University Press, 1996); Mayer, *Running on Race*.

18. Carmines and Stimson, *Issue Evolution*; Huckfeldt and Kohfeld, *Race and the Decline of Class in American Politics*; David C. Leege et al., *The Politics of Cultural Differences: Social Change and Voter Mobilization Strategies in the Post-New Deal Period* (Princeton, NJ: Princeton University Press, 2002); Mendelberg, *The Race Card*. For a good critique of this view, see Alan I. Abramowitz, "Issue Evolution Reconsidered: Racial Attitudes and Partisanship in the U.S. Electorate," *American Journal of Political Science* 38 (February 1994): 1–24.

19. Alan I. Abramowitz and Kyle L. Saunders, "Rational Hearts and Minds: Social Identity, Ideology, and Party Identification in the American Electorate" (paper presented at the Annual Meeting of the American Political Science Association, Chicago, IL, 2004).

20. Carmines and Stimson, *Issue Evolution*; Dawson, *Behind the Mule*; Fauntroy, *Republicans and the Black Vote*; Paul Frymer, *Uneasy Alliances: Race and Party Competition in America* (Princeton, NJ: Princeton University Press, 1999).

21. Rodolfo O. de la Garza, "Latino Politics," *Annual Review of Political Science* 7 (2004): 91–23; Louis DeSipio, *Counting on the Latino Vote: Latinos as a New Electorate* (Charlottesville, VA: University of Virginia Press, 1996); Rodney Hero et al., "Latino Participation, Partisanship, and Office Holding," *PS: Political Science and Politics* 33 (September 2000): 529–534.

22. Vincent L. Hutchings and Nicholas A. Valentino, "The Centrality of Race in American Politics," *Annual Review of Political Science* 7 (2004): 383–408.

23. The categories of white and non-white are created from *1948–2004 ANES Cumulative Data File* variable vcf0106. The white—non-Latino white—category is non-problematic. The same cannot be said for the non-white category. Lumping all non-whites into one category clearly is a less than desirable situation. However, the ANES simply does not have a large enough sample size to analyze racial and ethnic minorities separately. Perhaps the largest problem here arises from the rapidly growing Latino population in the United States. Latinos, of course, can and do identify in a number of different ways when it comes to race, and there has been a good deal of work done examining the issues surrounding Latino identity in American politics. Given the fact that Latinos are now the largest minority group in the United States, their importance politically will likely continue to rise, and thus so will academic research focused on the group. It is also likely that we will see additional work on the question of political coalitions between African Americans and Latinos. For some recent work in these areas, see R. Michael Alvarez and Lisa Garcia Bedolla, "The Foundations of Latino Voter Partisanship: Evidence from the 2000 Election," *Journal of Politics* 65 (February 2003): 31–49; de la Garza,

"Latino Politics"; Mary E. Campbell and Christabel L. Rogalin, "Categorical Imperatives: The Interaction of Latino and Racial Identification," *Social Science Quarterly* 87 (December 2006): 1030–1052; Matthew O. Hunt, "African American, Hispanic, and White Beliefs about Black/White Inequality, 1977–2004," *American Sociological Review* 72 (June 2007): 390–415; Karen M. Kaufmann, "Cracks in the Rainbow: Group Commonality as a Basis for Latino and African–American Political Coalitions," *Political Research Quarterly* 56 (June 2003): 199–210; Natalie Masuoka, "Defining the Group: Latino Identity and Political Participation," *American Politics Research* 36 (January 2008): 33–61; Kenneth J. Meier et al., "Divided or Together? Conflict and Cooperation between African Americans and Latinos," *Political Research Quarterly* 57 (September 2004): 399–409; Gabriel R. Sanchez, "Latino Group Consciousness and Perceptions of Commonality with African Americans," *Social Science Quarterly* 89 (June 2008): 428–444. Ideally, I would prefer to examine the party images of non-Latino whites, African Americans, and Latinos separately, but as noted above this is not possible in the ANES.

5 Party Images and Sex

1. In fact, a number of researchers argue that the gender gap is in reality due more to the behavior of men than to the behavior of women. See Thomas Byrne Edsall, *Building Red America: The New Conservative Coalition and the Drive for Permanent Power* (New York: Basic Books, 2006); Karen M. Kaufmann and John R. Petrocik, "The Changing Politics of American Men: Understanding the Sources of the Gender Gap," *American Journal of Political Science* 43 (July 1999): 864–887; Daniel Wirls, "Reinterpreting the Gender Gap," *Public Opinion Quarterly* 50 (autumn 1986): 316–330.

2. While the difference in Democratic presidential vote choice between men and women may not look as impressive as those based on family income and race presented in previous chapters, it must be noted that Figure 5.1 presents the gender gap within the electorate as a whole. If one were to present the gender gap among whites only, the difference between men and women would be larger due to the fact the non-whites (especially African Americans and, to a somewhat lesser extent, Latinos) are more Democratic than whites regardless of sex. The same, of course, could be said for the differences in presidential voting based on family income levels and church attendance.

3. Janet M. Box-Steffensmeier, Suzanna De Boef, and Tse-Min Lin, "The Dynamics of the Partisan Gender Gap," *American Political Science Review* 98 (August 2004): 515–528; Susan J. Carroll, "Voting Choices: Meet You at the Gender Gap," in *Gender and Elections: Shaping the Future of American Politics*, ed. Susan J. Carroll and Richard L. Fox (New York: Cambridge University Press, 2006), 74–96; Carole Kennedy Chaney, R. Michael Alvarez, and Jonathan Nagler, "Explaining the Gender Gap in U.S. Presidential Elections, 1980–1992," *Political Research Quarterly* 51 (June 1998): 311–339; Kathleen A. Frankovic, "Sex and Politics—New Alignments, Old Issues," *PS* 15 (summer 1982): 439–448; Jo Freeman, "Sex, Race, Religion, and Partisan Realignment," in *The Impact of Elections on Governing*, ed. Paul E. Scheele (Westport, CT: Praeger, 1999), 167–190; Susan E. Howell and Christine L. Day, "Complexities of the Gender Gap," *Journal of Politics* 62 (August 2000): 858–874; Ethel Klein, *Gender Politics: From Consciousness to Mass Politics* (Cambridge, MA: Harvard University Press, 1984); Carol M. Mueller, "The Empowerment of Women: Polling and the Women's Voting Bloc," in *The Politics of the Gender Gap: The*

Social Construction of Political Influence, ed. Carol M. Mueller (Newbury Park, CA: Sage Publications, 1988), 16–36; Carol M. Mueller, "The Gender Gap and Women's Political Influence," *Annals of the American Academy of Political and Social Science* 515 (May 1991): 23–37; Christina Wolbrecht, *The Politics of Women's Rights: Parties, Positions, and Change* (Princeton, NJ: Princeton University Press, 2000).

4. Kaufmann and Petrocik, "The Changing Politics of American Men: Understanding the Sources of the Gender Gap"; Barbara Norrander, "The Evolution of the Gender Gap," *Public Opinion Quarterly* 63 (winter 1999): 566–567; Richard A. Seltzer, Jody Newman, and Melissa Voorhees Leighton, *Sex as a Political Variable: Women as Candidates and Voters in U.S. Elections* (Boulder, CO: Lynne Rienner, 1997).

5. Karen M. Kaufmann, "Culture Wars, Secular Realignment, and the Gender Gap in Party Identification," *Political Behavior* 24 (September 2002): 283–307.

6. Henry C. Kenski, "The Gender Factor in a Changing Electorate," in *The Politics of the Gender Gap*, ed. Mueller, 38–60.

7. Carroll, "Voting Choices: Meet You at the Gender Gap"; Frankovic, "Sex and Politics—New Alignments, Old Issues"; Martin Gilens, "Gender and Support for Reagan: A Comprehensive Model of Presidential Approval," *American Journal of Political Science* 32 (February 1988): 19–49; Howell and Day, "Complexities of the Gender Gap"; Kenski, "The Gender Factor in a Changing Electorate"; Klein, *Gender Politics*; Ann Mari May and Kurt Stephenson, "Women and the Great Retrenchment: The Political Economy of Gender in the 1980s," *Journal of Economic Issues* 28 (June 1994): 533–542.

8. Anne M. Costain, "After Reagan: New Party Attitudes toward Gender," *Annals of the Academy of Political and Social Science* 515 (May 1991): 114–125, p. 121.

9. Carol Gilligan, *In a Different Voice: Psychological Theory and Women's Development* (Cambridge, MA: Harvard University Press, 1982), 100. For empirical evidence of this phenomenon, see Ann M. Beutel and Margaret Mooney Marini, "Gender and Values," *American Sociological Review* 60 (June 1995): 436–448.

10. Howell and Day, "Complexities of the Gender Gap"; Norrander, "The Evolution of the Gender Gap"; Robert Y. Shapiro and Harpeet Mahajan, "Gender Differences in Policy Preferences: A Summary of Trends from the 1960s to the 1980s," *Public Opinion Quarterly* 50 (spring 1986): 42–61.

11. R. Michael Alvarez and Edward J. McCaffery, "Are There Sex Differences in Fiscal Political Preferences?" *Political Research Quarterly* 56 (March 2003): 5–17; Kristi Andersen, "The Gender Gap and Experiences with the Welfare State," *PS: Political Science and Politics* 32 (March 1999): 17–19; Box-Steffensmeier et al., "The Dynamics of the Partisan Gender Gap"; Steven P. Erie and Martin Rein, "Women and the Welfare State," in *The Politics of the Gender Gap*, ed. Mueller, 173–191; Gilens, "Gender and Support for Reagan: A Comprehensive Model of Presidential Approval"; Karen Kaufmann, "The Partisan Paradox: Religious Commitment and the Gender Gap in Party Identification," *Public Opinion Quarterly* 68 (winter 2004): 491–511; Kaufmann and Petrocik, "The Changing Politics of American Men"; May and Stephenson, "Women and the Great Retrenchment: The Political Economy of Gender in the 1980s"; Mark Schlesinger and Caroline Heldman, "Gender Gap or Gender Gaps? New Perspectives on Support for Government Action and Policies," *Journal of Politics* 63 (February 2001): 59–92; Seltzer et al., *Sex as a Political Variable*.

12. Lynne M. Casper and Suzanne M. Bianchi, *Continuity and Change in the American Family* (Thousand Oaks, CA: Sage Publications, 2002).
13. Pamela Johnston Conover and Virginia Sapiro, "Gender, Feminist Consciousness, and War," *American Journal of Political Science* 37 (November 1993): 1079–1099; Frankovic, "Sex and Politics—New Alignments, Old Issues"; Gilens, "Gender and Support for Reagan: A Comprehensive Model of Presidential Approval"; Shapiro and Mahajan, "Gender Differences in Policy Preferences: A Summary of Trends from the 1960s to the 1980s"; Tom W. Smith, "The Polls: Gender and Attitudes toward Violence," *Public Opinion Quarterly* 48 (spring 1984): 384–396. It should be noted that Frankovic also finds views on environmental issues to be partially responsible for the gender gap, an argument that is not addressed in this study.
14. Much more will be said on the culture war in the next chapter.
15. Freeman, "Sex, Race, Religion, and Realignment"; Kaufmann, "Culture Wars, Secular Realignment, and the Gender Gap in Party Identification"; Klein, *Gender Politics*; Wolbrecht, *The Politics of Women's Rights*.
16. Pamela Johnston Conover, "Feminists and the Gender Gap," *Journal of Politics* 50 (November 1988): 985–1010. For the opposing side of this argument, see Elizabeth Ardell Cook and Clyde Wilcox, "Feminism and the Gender Gap: A Second Look," *Journal of Politics* 53 (November 1991): 1111–1122.
17. Carroll, "Voting Choices: Meet You at the Gender Gap"; Chaney et al., "Explaining the Gender Gap in U.S. Presidential Elections."
18. Mark D. Brewer and Jeffrey M. Stonecash, *Split: Class and Cultural Divides in American Politics* (Washington, DC: CQ Press, 2007); Costain, "After Reagan: New Party Attitudes toward Gender"; Freeman, "Sex, Race, Religion, and Partisan Realignment"; John Gerring, *Party Ideologies in America, 1828–1996* (New York: Cambridge University Press, 1998); Klein, *Gender Politics*; Geoffrey Layman, *The Great Divide: Religious and Cultural Conflict in American Party Politics* (New York: Columbia University Press, 2001); Kira Sanbonmatsu, *Democrats, Republicans, and the Politics of Women's Place* (Ann Arbor, MI: University of Michigan Press, 2002); Wolbrecht, *The Politics of Women's Rights*.

6 Party Images and Religious Salience

1. James L. Guth and John C. Green, "Salience: The Core Concept?" in *Rediscovering the Religious Factor in American Politics*, ed. David C. Leege and Lyman A. Kellstedt (Armonk, NY: M.E. Sharpe), 157–174. See also Charles Y. Glock and Rodney Stark, *Religion and Society in Tension* (Chicago: Rand McNally and Company, 1965), ch. 2.
2. Mark D. Brewer, *Relevant No More? The Catholic/Protestant Divide in American Electoral Politics* (Lanham, MD: Lexington Books, 2003); Paul Kleppner, *The Third Electoral System, 1853–1892* (Chapel Hill, NC: University of North Carolina Press, 1979); Everett Carll Ladd, Jr., with Charles D. Hadley, *Transformations of the American Party System* (New York: W.W. Norton, 1975).
3. Pippa Norris and Ronald Inglehart, *Sacred and Secular: Religion and Politics Worldwide* (New York: Cambridge University Press, 2004).
4. Joan Del Fattore, *The Fourth R: Conflicts Over Religion in America's Public Schools* (New Haven, CT: Yale University Press, 2004); Kenneth M. Dolbeare and Phillip E. Hammond, *The School Prayer Decisions: From Court Policy to Local Practice* (Chicago: University of Chicago Press, 1971); H. Frank Way, Jr., "Survey Research on Judicial Decisions: The Prayer and Bible Reading Cases," *Western Political Quarterly* 21 (June 1968): 189–205.

5. Barry D. Adam, *The Rise of a Gay and Lesbian Movement*, rev. ed. (Boston: Twayne Publishers, 1995); David Allyn, *Make Love, Not War: The Sexual Revolution* (Boston: Little, Brown, and Company, 2000).

6. Ethel Klein, *Gender Politics: From Consciousness to Mass Politics* (Cambridge, MA: Harvard University Press, 1984); Kira Sanbonmatsu, *Democrats, Republicans, and the Politics of Women's Place* (Ann Arbor, MI: University of Michigan Press, 2002); Christina Wolbrecht, *The Politics of Women's Rights: Parties, Positions, and Change* (Princeton, NJ: Princeton University Press, 2000).

7. Mark Abrahamson, *Out-of-wedlock Births: The United States in Comparative Perspective* (Westport, CT: Praeger, 1998); Lynne M. Casper and Suzanne M. Bianchi, *Continuity and Change in the American Family* (Thousand Oaks, CA: Sage Publications, 2002).

8. Mark D. Brewer and Jeffrey M. Stonecash, *Split: Class and Cultural Divides in American Politics* (Washington, DC: CQ Press, 2007).

9. Robert Wuthnow, *The Restructuring of American Religion: Society and Faith Since World War II* (Princeton, NJ: Princeton University Press, 1988); Robert Wuthnow, *The Struggle for America's Soul: Evangelicals, Liberals, and Secularism* (Grand Rapids, MI: William B. Eerdmans Publishing Company, 1989).

10. James Davison Hunter, *Culture Wars: The Struggle to Define America* (New York: Basic Books, 1991), 34.

11. Hunter, *Culture Wars*, 42.

12. Hunter, *Culture Wars*. See also James Davison Hunter, *Before the Shooting Begins: Searching for Democracy in America's Culture War* (New York: The Free Press, 1994).

13. Nancy J. Davis and Robert V. Robinson, "Religious Orthodoxy in American Society: The Myth of a Monolithic Camp," *Journal for the Scientific Study of Religion* 35 (September 1996): 229–245; Nancy J. Davis and Robert V. Robinson, "Are Rumors of War Exaggerated? Religious Orthodoxy and Moral Progressivism in America," *American Journal of Sociology* 102 (November 1996): 756–787; Paul DiMaggio, John Evans, and Bethany Bryson, "Have Americans' Social Attitudes Become More Polarized?" *American Journal of Sociology* 102 (November 1996): 690–755; Rhys Williams, ed., *Cultural Wars in American Politics: Critical Reviews of a Popular Myth* (New York: Aldine de Gruyter, 1997).

14. Greg D. Adams, "Abortion: Evidence of an Issue Evolution," *American Journal of Political Science* 41 (July 1997): 718–737; John H. Evans, "Have Americans' Attitudes Become More Polarized?—An Update," *Social Science Quarterly* 84 (March 2003): 71–90; Dale McConkey, "Whither Hunter's Culture War? Shifts in Evangelical Morality, 1988–1998," *Sociology of Religion* 62 (summer 2001): 149–174. Michael Emerson demonstrated that differences on the issue of abortion could be traced to divergent views of moral authority, supporting Hunter's original argument. Michael O. Emerson, "Through Tinted Glasses: Religion, Worldviews, and Abortion Attitudes," *Journal for the Scientific Study of Religion* 35 (March 1996): 41–55.

15. Clem Brooks, "Religious Influence and the Politics of Family Decline Concern: Trends, Sources, and U.S. Political Behavior," *American Sociological Review* 67 (April 2002): 191–211.

16. Geoffrey C. Layman, " 'Culture Wars' in the American Party System: Religious and Cultural Change among Partisan Activists since 1972," *American Politics Quarterly* 27 (January 1999): 89–121; Geoffrey Layman, *The Great Divide: Religious and Cultural Conflict in American Party Politics* (New York: Columbia University Press, 2001). See also David C. Leege et al., *The Politics of Cultural Differences* (Princeton, NJ: Princeton University Press, 2002).

17. Alan I. Abramowitz, "It's Abortion, Stupid: Policy Voting in the 1992 Presidential Election," *Journal of Politics* 57 (February 1995): 176–186; Adams, "Abortion: Evidence of an Issue Evolution"; R. Michael Alvarez and Jonathan Nagler, "Economics, Issues, and the Perot Candidacy: Voter Choice in the 1992 Presidential Election," *American Journal of Political Science* 39 (August 1995): 714–744; R. Michael Alvarez and Jonathan Nagler, "Economics, Entitlements, and Social Issues: Voter Choice in the 1996 Presidential Election," *American Journal of Political Science* 42 (October 1998): 1349–1363.

18. Brewer, *Relevant No More?*; Andrew Kohut et al., *The Diminishing Divide: Religion's Changing Role in American Politics* (Washington, DC: The Brookings Institution, 2000); Geoffrey C. Layman, "Religion and Political Behavior in the United States: The Impact of Beliefs, Affiliations, and Commitment from 1980–1984," *Public Opinion Quarterly* 61 (summer 1997): 288–316; Geoffrey C. Layman, *The Great Divide*; Geoffrey C. Layman and Edward G. Carmines, "Cultural Conflict in American Politics: Religious Traditionalism, Postmaterialism, and U.S. Political Behavior," *Journal of Politics* 59 (August 1997): 751–777.

19. Chip Berlet and Matthew N. Lyons, *Right-wing Populism in America: Too Close for Comfort* (New York: Guilford Press, 2000); Brewer and Stonecash, *Split*; Thomas Byrne Edsall, with Mary D. Edsall, *Chain Reaction: The Impact of Race, Rights, and Taxes on American Politics* (New York: W.W. Norton, 1991); John Gerring, *Party Ideologies in America, 1828–1996* (New York: Cambridge University Press, 1998); Jonathan Knuckey, "A New Front in the Culture War? Moral Traditionalism and Voting Behavior in U.S. House Elections," *American Politics Research* 33 (September 2005): 645–671; Layman, *The Great Divide*; John Micklethwait and Adrian Wooldridge, *The Right Nation: Conservative Power in America* (New York: Penguin Press, 2004); Byron Shafer, "The New Cultural Politics," *PS* 18 (spring 1985): 221–231; John Kenneth White, *The Values Divide: American Politics and Culture in Transition* (New York: Chatham House Publishers, 2003).

20. Guth and Green, "Salience: The Core Concept?"; Kenneth D. Wald and Corwin E. Smidt, "Measurement Strategies in the Study of Religion and Politics," in *Rediscovering the Religious Factor in American Politics*, ed. David C. Leege and Lyman A. Kellstedt (Armonk, NY: M.E. Sharpe, 1993), 26–49.

21. Luckily, analysis shows that the inability to use the religious guidance question likely does not matter much, at least for the work being done here. Comparing the results presented in the text of this chapter generated using church attendance along with results generated by creating a religious salience index based on church attendance and religious guidance reveals a remarkable degree of similarity. Indeed, they are so similar that it is difficult to tell them apart.

22. For 1952–1968 church attendance is derived from the *1948–2004 ANES Cumulative Data File* variable number vcf0131. Those who reported going to church "regularly" are coded as high attenders, those who reported going "often" are moderate attenders, and those who reported going "seldom," "never," or who stated they had no religious preference (1960–1968 only) are coded as low attenders. For 1972–2004 church attendance is derived from variable vcf0130. Those who reported going to church "every week" are coded high attenders, those who reported going "almost every week" or "once or twice a month" are coded moderate attenders, and those who reported going "a few times a year," "never," or who stated they had no religious preference (1972–1988 only) are coded as low attenders.

7 Conclusion

1. For a discussion of this era in American politics, see Michael E. McGerr, *The Decline of Popular Politics: The American North, 1865–1928* (New York: Oxford University Press, 1986).
2. Robert S. Erikson, Michael B. MacKuen, and James A. Stimson, *The Macro Polity* (New York: Cambridge University Press, 2002).
3. Walter Lippmann, *Public Opinion* (New York: Harcourt Brace Jovanovich, 1922); James A. Stimson, *Tides of Consent: How Public Opinion Shapes American Politics* (New York: Cambridge University Press, 2004); John R. Zaller, *The Nature and Origins of Mass Opinion* (New York: Cambridge University Press, 1992).
4. Mark D. Brewer and Jeffrey M. Stonecash, *Dynamics of American Political Parties* (New York: Cambridge University Press, forthcoming).
5. David C. Leege et al., *The Politics of Cultural Differences: Social Change and Voter Mobilization Strategies in the Post-New Deal Period* (Princeton, NJ: Princeton University Press, 2002).
6. John R. Petrocik, "Issue Ownership in Presidential Elections, with a 1980 Case Study," *American Journal of Political Science* 40 (August 1996): 825–850; John R. Petrocik, William L. Benoit, and Glenn J. Hansen, "Issue Ownership and Presidential Campaigning, 1952–2000," *Political Science Quarterly* 118 (December 2003): 599–626.
7. Donald Green, Bradley Palmquist, and Eric Schickler, *Partisan Hearts and Minds: Political Parties and the Social Identities of Voters* (New Haven, CT: Yale University Press, 2002).
8. E. E. Schattschneider, *Party Government* (New York: Holt, Rinehart, and Winston, 1942), 48.
9. As noted in the Preface, the term "pictures in our heads" is from Lippmann's *Public Opinion*.

Bibliography

Abrahamson, Mark. 1998. *Out-of-wedlock Births: The United States in Comparative Perspective*. Westport, CT: Praeger.

Abramowitz, Alan I. 1994. "Issue Evolution Reconsidered: Racial Attitudes and Partisanship in the U.S. Electorate." *American Journal of Political Science* 38 (February): 1–24.

——. 1995. "It's Abortion, Stupid: Policy Voting in the 1992 Presidential Election." *Journal of Politics* 57 (February): 176–186.

Abramowitz, Alan I., and Kyle L. Saunders. 1998. "Ideological Realignment in the U.S. Electorate." *Journal of Politics* 60 (August): 634–652.

——. 2004. "Rational Hearts and Minds: Social Identity, Ideology, and Party Identification in the American Electorate." Paper presented at the Annual Meeting of the American Political Science Association. Chicago.

——. 2005. "Why Can't We All Just Get Along? The Reality of a Polarized America." *The Forum* 3.

Adam, Barry D. 1995. *The Rise of a Gay and Lesbian Movement*, revised edition. Boston: Twayne Publishers.

Adams, Greg D. 1997. "Abortion: Evidence of an Issue Evolution." *American Journal of Political Science* 41 (July): 718–737.

Aldrich, John H. 1999. "Political Parties in a Critical Era." *American Politics Quarterly* 27 (January): 9–32.

——. 2003. "Electoral Democracy during Politics as Usual—and Unusual." In *Electoral Democracy*, edited by Michael B. MacKuen and George Rabinowitz, 270–310. Ann Arbor, MI: University of Michigan Press.

Allyn, David. 2000. *Make Love, Not War: The Sexual Revolution*. Boston: Little, Brown, and Company.

Alvarez, R. Michael, and Lisa Garcia Bedolla. 2003. "The Foundations of Latino Voter Partisanship: Evidence from the 2000 Election." *Journal of Politics* 65 (February): 31–49.

Alvarez, R. Michael, and John Brehm. 1997. "Are Americans Ambivalent Towards Racial Policies?" *American Journal of Political Science* 41 (April): 345–374.

Alvarez, R. Michael, and Edward J. McCaffery. 2003. "Are There Sex Differences in Fiscal Political Preferences?" *Political Research Quarterly* 56 (March): 5–17.

Alvarez, R. Michael, and Jonathan Nagler. 1995. "Economics, Issues, and the Perot

Candidacy: Voter Choice in the 1992 Presidential Election." *American Journal of Political Science* 39 (August): 714–744.

——. 1998. "Economics, Entitlements, and Social Issues: Voter Choice in the 1996 Presidential Election." *American Journal of Political Science* 42 (October): 1349–1363.

American National Election Studies. 2005. *The 1948–2004 ANES Cumulative Data File* [dataset]. Stanford University and University of Michigan [producers and distributors].

Andersen, Kristi. 1999. "The Gender Gap and Experiences with the Welfare State." *PS: Political Science and Politics* 32 (March): 17–19.

Baer, Kenneth S. 2000. *Reinventing Democrats: The Politics of Liberalism from Reagan to Clinton.* Lawrence, KS: University Press of Kansas.

Barker, Lucius J., and Mack H. Jones. 1994. *African Americans and the American Political System*, 3rd edition. Englewood Cliffs, NJ: Prentice Hall.

Bartels, Larry M. 1998. "Electoral Continuity and Change, 1868–1996." *Electoral Studies* 17 (September): 301–326.

——. 2000. "Partisanship and Voting Behavior, 1952–1996." *American Journal of Political Science* 44 (January): 35–50.

——. 2006. "What's the Matter with *What's the Matter with Kansas?*" *Quarterly Journal of Political Science* 1 (March): 201–226.

Baumer, Donald C., and Howard J. Gold. 1995. "Party Images and the American Electorate." *American Politics Quarterly* 23 (January): 33–61.

——. 2002. "Party Images After the Clinton Years." Paper presented at the Annual Meeting of the New England Political Science Association. Portland, ME.

Berelson, Bernard R., Paul F. Lazarsfeld, and William N. McPhee. 1954. *Voting: A Study of Opinion Formation in a Presidential Campaign.* Chicago: University of Chicago Press.

Berlet, Chip, and Matthew N. Lyons. 2000. *Right-wing Populism in America: Too Close for Comfort.* New York: Guilford Press.

Bernstein, Jared, Elizabeth McNichol, and Karen Lyons. 2006. "Pulling Apart: A State-by-state Analysis of Income Trends." Washington, DC: Center on Budget and Policy Priorities and Economic Policy Institute.

Beutel, Ann M., and Margaret Mooney Marini. 1995. "Gender and Values." *American Sociological Review* 60 (June): 436–448.

Bobo, Lawrence. 1988. "Group Conflict, Prejudice, and the Paradox of Contemporary Racial Attitudes." In *Eliminating Racism: Profiles in Controversy*, edited by Phyllis A. Katz and Dalmas A. Taylor, 85–114. New York: Plenum Press.

Bobo, Lawrence, and James R. Klugel. 1993. "Opposition to Race Targeting: Self Interest, Stratification Ideology, or Racial Attitudes." *American Sociological Review* 58 (August): 443–464.

Bond, Jon R., and Richard Fleisher, eds. 2000. *Polarized Politics: Congress and the President in a Partisan Era.* Washington, DC: CQ Press.

Box-Steffensmeier, Janet M., Suzanna De Boef, and Tse-Min Lin. 2004. "The Dynamics of the Partisan Gender Gap." *American Political Science Review* 98 (August): 515–528.

Brady, Henry E., and Paul M. Sniderman. 1985. "Attitude Attribution: A Group Basis for Political Reasoning." *American Political Science Review* 79 (December): 1061–1078.

Brewer, Mark D. 2003. *Relevant No More? The Catholic/Protestant Divide in American Electoral Politics.* Lanham, MD: Lexington Books.

——— . 2005. "The Rise of Partisanship and the Expansion of Partisan Conflict within the American Electorate." *Political Research Quarterly* 58 (June): 219–229.

Brewer, Mark D., and Jeffrey M. Stonecash. 2007. *Split: Class and Cultural Divides in American Politics.* Washington, DC: CQ Press.

——— . Forthcoming. *Dynamics of American Political Parties.* New York: Cambridge University Press.

Broder, David S. 1972. *The Party's Over: The Failure of Politics in America.* New York: Harper and Row.

Brooks, Clem. 2002. "Religious Influence and the Politics of Family Decline Concern: Trends, Sources, and U.S. Political Behavior." *American Sociological Review* 67 (April): 191–211.

Bryce, James. 1959. *The American Commonwealth,* 2 vols. New York: G.P. Putnam and Sons.

Campbell, Angus, Philip E. Converse, Warren E. Miller, and Donald E. Stokes. 1960. *The American Voter.* New York: John Wiley and Sons.

Campbell, Mary E., and Christabel L. Rogalin. 2006. "Categorical Imperatives: The Interaction of Latino and Racial Identification." *Social Science Quarterly* 87 (December): 1030–1052.

Carmines, Edward G., and Geoffrey C. Layman. 1997. "Issue Evolution in Postwar American Politics: Old Certainties and Fresh Tensions." In *Present Discontents: American Politics in the Very Late Twentieth Century,* edited by Byron E. Shafer, 89–134. Chatham, NJ: Chatham House Publishers.

Carmines, Edward G., Steven H. Renten, and James A. Stimson. 1984. "Events and Alignments: The Party Image Link." In *Controversies in Voting Behavior,* 2nd edition, edited by Richard G. Niemi and Herbert F. Weisberg, 545–560. Washington, DC: CQ Press.

Carmines, Edward G., and James A. Stimson. 1989. *Issue Evolution: Race and the Transformation of American Politics.* Princeton, NJ: Princeton University Press.

Carroll, Susan J. 2006. "Voting Choices: Meet You at the Gender Gap." In *Gender and Elections: Shaping the Future of American Politics,* edited by Susan J. Carroll and Richard L. Fox, 74–96. New York: Cambridge University Press.

Carter, Dan T. 1996. *From George Wallace to Newt Gingrich: Race in the Conservative Counterrevolution.* Baton Rouge, LA: Louisiana State University Press.

Casper, Lynne M., and Suzanne M. Bianchi. 2002. *Continuity and Change in the American Family.* Thousand Oaks, CA: Sage Publications.

Ceaser, James W. 1984. "The Theory of Governance of the Reagan Administration." In *The Reagan Presidency and the Governing of America,* edited by Lester M. Salamon and Michael S. Lund, 57–87. Washington, DC: The Urban Institute Press.

Chaney, Carole Kennedy, R. Michael Alvarez, and Jonathan Nagler. 1998. "Explaining the Gender Gap in U.S. Presidential Elections, 1980–1992." *Political Research Quarterly* 51 (June): 311–339.

Conover, Pamela Johnston. 1988. "Feminists and the Gender Gap." *Journal of Politics* 50 (November): 985–1010.

Conover, Pamela Johnston, and Stanley Feldman. 1986. "The Role of Inference in the Perception of Political Candidates." In *Political Cognition*, edited by Richard R. Lau and David O. Sears, 127–158. Hillsdale, NJ: Lawrence Erlbaum Associates.

———. 1989. "Candidate Perception in an Ambiguous World: Campaigns, Cues, and Inference Processes." *American Journal of Political Science* 33 (November): 912–940.

Conover, Pamela Johnston, and Virginia Sapiro. 1993. "Gender, Feminist Consciousness, and War." *American Journal of Political Science* 37 (November): 1079–1099.

Cook, Elizabeth Ardell, and Clyde Wilcox. 1991. "Feminism and the Gender Gap: A Second Look." *Journal of Politics* 53 (November): 1111–1122.

Costain, Anne M. 1991. "After Reagan: New Party Attitudes toward Gender." *Annals of the Academy of Political and Social Science* 515 (May): 114–125.

Craig, Steven C. 1985. "The Decline of Partisanship in the United States: A Reexamination of the Neutrality Hypothesis." *Political Behavior* 7 (March): 57–78.

Danziger, Sheldon, and Peter Gottschalk. 1995. *America Unequal*. Cambridge, MA: Harvard University Press.

Davis, Nancy J., and Robert V. Robinson. 1996. "Religious Orthodoxy in American Society: The Myth of a Monolithic Camp." *Journal for the Scientific Study of Religion* 35 (September): 229–245.

———. 1996. "Are the Rumors of War Exaggerated? Religious Orthodoxy and Moral Progressivism in America." *American Journal of Sociology* 102 (November): 756–787.

Dawson, Michael C. 1994. *Behind the Mule: Race and Class in African–American Politics*. Princeton, NJ: Princeton University Press.

de la Garza, Rodolfo O. 2004. "Latino Politics." *Annual Review of Political Science* 7: 91–123.

Del Fattore, Joan. 2004. *The Fourth R: Conflicts over Religion in America's Public Schools*. New Haven, CT: Yale University Press.

DeSipio, Louis. 1996. *Counting on the Latino Vote: Latinos as a New Electorate*. Charlottesville, VA: University of Virginia Press.

DiMaggio, Paul, John Evans, and Bethany Bryson. 1996. "Have Americans' Social Attitudes Become More Polarized?" *American Journal of Sociology* 102 (November): 690–755.

Dolbeare, Kenneth M., and Phillip E. Hammond. 1971. *The School Prayer Decisions: From Court Policy to Local Practice*. Chicago: University of Chicago Press.

Edsall, Thomas Byrne. 2006. *Building Red America: The New Conservative Coalition and the Drive for Permanent Power*. New York: Basic Books.

Edsall, Thomas Byrne, with Mary D. Edsall. 1991. *Chain Reaction: The Impact of Race, Rights, and Taxes on American Politics*. New York: W.W. Norton & Company.

Emerson, Michael O. 1996. "Through Tinted Glasses: Religion, Worldviews, and Abortion Attitudes." *Journal for the Scientific Study of Religion* 35 (March): 41–55.

Erie, Steven P., and Martin Rein. 1988. "Women and the Welfare State." In *The Politics of the Gender Gap: The Social Construction of Social Influence*, edited by Carol M. Mueller, 173–191. Newbury Park, CA: Sage Publications.

Erikson Robert S., Thomas D. Lancaster, and David W. Romero. 1989. "Group Components of the Presidential Vote, 1952–1984." *Journal of Politics* 51 (May): 337–346.

Erikson, Robert S., Michael B. MacKuen, and James A. Stimson. 2002. *The Macro Polity*. New York: Cambridge University Press.

Evans, John H. 2003. "Have Americans' Attitudes Become More Polarized?—An Update." *Social Science Quarterly* 84 (March): 71–90.

Fauntroy, Michael K. 2007. *Republicans and the Black Vote*. Boulder, CO: Lynne Rienner.

Fiorina, Morris P. 1981. *Retrospective Voting in American National Elections*. New Haven, CT: Yale University Press.

Fiorina, Morris P., with Samuel J. Abrams and Jeremy C. Pope. 2006. *Culture War? The Myth of a Polarized America*. New York: Pearson/Longman.

Frank, Thomas. 2004. *What's the Matter with Kansas? How Conservatives Won the Heart of America*. New York: Henry Holt and Company.

Frankovic, Kathleen A. 1982. "Sex and Politics—New Alignments, Old Issues." *PS: Political Science & Politics* 15 (summer): 439–448.

Freeman, Jo. 1986. "The Political Culture of the Democratic and Republican Parties." *Political Science Quarterly* 101 (3): 327–356.

———. 1999. "Sex, Race, Religion, and Partisan Realignment." In *The Impact of Elections on Governing*, edited by Paul E. Scheele, 167–190. Westport, CT: Praeger.

Frymer, Paul. 1999. *Uneasy Alliances: Race and Party Competition in America*. Princeton, NJ: Princeton University Press.

Geer, John G. 1988. "What Do Open-ended Questions Measure?" *Public Opinion Quarterly* 52 (autumn): 365–371.

———. 1991. "Critical Realignments and the Public Opinion Poll." *Journal of Politics* 53 (May): 434–453.

———. 1991. "The Electorate's Partisan Evaluations: Evidence of a Continuing Democratic Edge." *Public Opinion Quarterly* 55 (summer): 218–231.

———. 1991. "Do Open-ended Questions Measure 'Salient' Issues?" *Public Opinion Quarterly* 55 (autumn): 360–370.

Gerring, John. 1998. *Party Ideologies in America, 1828–1996*. New York: Cambridge University Press.

Gilens, Martin. 1988. "Gender and Support for Reagan: A Comprehensive Model of Presidential Approval." *American Journal of Political Science* 32 (February): 19–49.

———. 1998. "Racial Attitudes and Race-neutral Social Policies: White Opposition to Welfare and the Politics of Racial Inequality." In *Perception and Prejudice: Race and Politics in the United States*, edited by Jon Hurwitz and Mark Peffley, 171–201. New Haven, CT: Yale University Press.

———. 1999. *Why Americans Hate Welfare: Race, Media, and the Politics of Antipoverty Policy*. Chicago: University of Chicago Press.

Gilligan, Carol. 1982. *In a Different Voice: Psychological Theory and Women's Development*. Cambridge, MA: Harvard University Press.

Glaeser, Edward L. 2005. "Inequality." *National Bureau of Economic Research Working Paper No. 11511*. Cambridge, MA.

Glaser, James M. 1995. "Black and White Perceptions of Party Differences." *Political Behavior* 17 (June): 155–177.

Glock, Charles Y., and Rodney Stark. 1965. *Religion and Society in Tension.* Chicago: Rand McNally and Company.

Goodwyn, Lawrence. 1976. *Democratic Promise: The Populist Moment in America.* New York: Oxford University Press.

Green, Donald, Bradley Palmquist, and Eric Schickler. 2002. *Partisan Hearts and Minds: Political Parties and the Social Identities of Voters.* New Haven, CT: Yale University Press.

Groseclose, Tim, Steven D. Levitt, and James M. Snyder. 1999. "Comparing Interest Group Scores Across Time and Chambers: Adjusted ADA Scores for the U.S. Congress." *American Political Science Review* 93 (March): 33–50.

Guth, James L., and John C. Green. 1993. "Salience: The Core Concept?" In *Rediscovering the Religious Factor in American Politics*, edited by David C. Leege and Lyman A. Kellstedt, 157–174. Armonk, NY: M.E. Sharpe.

Hamilton, Richard F. 1972. *Class and Politics in the United States.* New York: John Wiley & Sons.

Hartz, Louis. 1955. *The Liberal Tradition in America.* New York: Harcourt, Brace, and World.

Hays, Samuel P. 1964. "The Politics of Reform in Municipal Government in the Progressive Era." *Pacific Northwest Quarterly* 55 (October): 157–169.

Hero, Rodney, F. Chris Garcia, John Garcia, and Harry Pachon. 2000. "Latino Participation, Partisanship, and Office Holding." *PS: Political Science and Politics* 33 (September): 529–534.

Hetherington, Marc J. 2001. "Resurgent Mass Partisanship: The Role of Elite Polarization." *American Political Science Review* 95 (September): 619–631.

Hicks, John D. 1931. *The Populist Revolt.* Minneapolis, MN: University of Minnesota Press.

Howell, Susan E., and Christine L. Day. 2000. "Complexities of the Gender Gap." *Journal of Politics* 62 (August): 858–874.

Huckfeldt, Robert, and Carol Weitzel Kohfeld. 1989. *Race and the Decline of Class in American Politics.* Urbana, IL: University of Illinois Press.

Hughes, Michael. 1997. "Symbolic Racism, Old-fashioned Racism, and Whites' Opposition to Affirmative Action." In *Racial Attitudes in the 1990s: Continuity and Change*, edited by Steven A. Tuch and Jack K. Martin, 46–75. Westport, CT: Praeger.

Hunt, Matthew O. 2007. "African American, Hispanic, and White Beliefs about Black/White Inequality, 1977–2004." *American Sociological Review* 72 (June): 390–415.

Hunter, James Davison. 1991. *Culture Wars: The Struggle to Define America.* New York: Basic Books.

——— . 1994. *Before the Shooting Begins: Searching for Democracy in America's Culture War.* New York: The Free Press.

Hurwitz, Jon, and Mark Peffley. 1998. "Introduction." In *Perception and Prejudice: Race and Politics in the United States*, edited by Jon Hurwitz and Mark Peffley, 1–16. New Haven, CT: Yale University Press.

Hutchings, Vincent L. 2003. *Public Opinion and Democratic Accountability: How Citizens Learn about Politics.* Princeton, NJ: Princeton University Press.

Hutchings, Vincent L., and Nicholas A. Valentino. 2004. "The Centrality of Race in American Politics." *Annual Review of Political Science* 7: 383–408.

Inglehart, Ronald. 1977. *The Silent Revolution: Changing Values and Political Styles among Western Publics.* Princeton, NJ: Princeton University Press.

———. 1981. "Post-materialism in an Environment of Insecurity." *American Political Science Review* 75 (December): 880–900.

———. 1990. *Culture Shift in Advanced Industrial Society.* Princeton, NJ: Princeton University Press.

———. 1997. *Modernization and Postmodernization: Cultural, Economic, and Political Change in 43 Societies.* Princeton, NJ: Princeton University Press.

Jackman, Mary R. 1994. *The Velvet Glove: Paternalism and Conflict in Gender, Class, and Race Relations.* Berkeley, CA: University of California Press.

Jackman, Mary R., and Robert W. Jackman. 1983. *Class Awareness in the United States.* Berkeley, CA: University of California Press.

Jacobson, Gary C. 2000. "The Electoral Basis of Polarization in Congress." Paper presented at the Annual Meeting of the American Political Science Association, Washington, DC.

———. 2001. "A House and Senate Divided: The Clinton Legacy and the Congressional Elections of 2000." *Political Science Quarterly* 116 (spring): 5–27.

———. 2007. *A Divider, Not a Uniter: George W. Bush and the American People.* New York: Pearson/Longman.

Jacoby, William G. 1988. "The Impact of Party Identification on Issue Attitudes." *American Journal of Political Science* 32 (August): 643–661.

Jamieson, Kathleen Hall. 1992. *Dirty Politics: Deception, Distraction, and Democracy.* New York: Oxford University Press.

Jarvis, Sharon E. 2005. *The Talk of the Party: Political Labels, Symbolic Capital, and American Life.* Lanham, MD: Rowman & Littlefield Publishers.

Judd, Dennis R., and Todd Swanstrom. 2008. *City Politics: The Political Economy of Urban America,* 6th edition. New York: Pearson/Longman.

Kaufmann, Karen M. 2002. "Culture Wars, Secular Realignment, and the Gender Gap in Party Identification." *Political Behavior* 24 (September): 283–307.

———. 2003. "Cracks in the Rainbow: Group Commonality as a Basis for Latino and African–American Political Coalitions." *Political Research Quarterly* 56 (June): 199–210.

———. 2004. "The Partisan Paradox: Religious Commitment and the Gender Gap in Party Identification." *Public Opinion Quarterly* 68 (winter): 491–511.

Kaufmann, Karen M., and John R. Petrocik. 1999. "The Changing Politics of American Men: Understanding the Sources of the Gender Gap." *American Journal of Political Science* 43 (July): 864–887.

Kelley, Stanley. 1983. *Interpreting Elections.* Princeton, NJ: Princeton University Press.

Kenski, Henry C. 1988. "The Gender Factor in a Changing Electorate." In *The Politics of the Gender Gap: The Social Construction of Political Influence,* edited by Carol M. Mueller, 38–60. Newbury Park, CA: Sage Publications.

Key, V.O., Jr. 1961. *Public Opinion and American Democracy.* New York: Alfred A. Knopf.

———. 1984. *Southern Politics in State and Nation,* new edition. Knoxville, TN: University of Tennessee Press.

Key, V.O., Jr., with the assistance of Milton C. Cummings, Jr. 1966. *The Responsible Electorate: Rationality in Presidential Voting, 1936–1960.* Cambridge, MA: Harvard University Press.

Kimball, David C. 2005. "Priming Partisan Evaluations of Congress." *Legislative Studies Quarterly* 30 (February): 63–84.

Kinder, Donald R., and Tali Mendelberg. 2000. "Individualism Reconsidered: Principles and Prejudice in Contemporary American Opinion," In *Racialized Politics: The Debate About Racism in America,* edited by David O. Sears, Jim Sidanius, and Lawrence Bobo, 44–74. Chicago: University of Chicago Press.

Kinder, Donald R., and Lynn M. Sanders. 1996. *Divided by Color: Racial Politics and Democratic Ideals.* Chicago: University of Chicago Press.

Kinder, Donald R., and David O. Sears. 1981. "Prejudice and Politics: Symbolic Racism Versus Racial Threats to the Good Life." *Journal of Personality and Social Psychology* 40 (March): 414–431.

Kinder, Donald R., and Nicholas Winter. 2001. "Exploring the Racial Divide: Blacks, Whites, and Opinion on National Policy." *American Journal of Political Science* 45 (April): 439–456.

King, Martin Luther, Jr. 1968. "I've Been to the Mountaintop." Memphis, TN.

Klein, Ethel. 1984. *Gender Politics: From Consciousness to Mass Politics.* Cambridge, MA: Harvard University Press.

Kleppner, Paul. 1979. *The Third Electoral System, 1853–1892.* Chapel Hill, NC: University of North Carolina Press.

Knuckey, Jonathan. 2005. "A New Front in the Culture War? Moral Traditionalism and Voting Behavior in U.S. House Elections." *American Politics Research* 33 (September): 645–671.

——. 2006. "Explaining Recent Changes in the Partisan Identifications of Southern Whites." *Political Research Quarterly* 59 (March): 57–70.

Kohut, Andrew, John C. Green, Scott Keeter, and Robert C. Toth. 2000. *The Diminishing Divide: Religion's Changing Role in American Politics.* Washington, DC: The Brookings Institution.

Konda, Thomas M., and Lee Sigelman. 1987. "Public Evaluations of the American Parties, 1952–1984." *Journal of Politics* 49 (August): 814–829.

Ladd, Everett Carll, Jr. 1978. *Where Have All the Voters Gone? The Fracturing of America's Political Parties.* New York: W.W. Norton & Company.

Ladd, Everett Carll, Jr., with Charles D. Hadley. 1975. *Transformations of the American Party System.* New York: W.W. Norton.

Lawrence, David G. 1991. "The Collapse of the Democratic Majority: Economics and Vote Choice since 1952." *Western Political Quarterly* 44 (December): 797–820.

——. 1996. *The Collapse of the Democratic Presidential Majority.* Boulder, CO: Westview Press.

Layman, Geoffrey C. 1997. "Religion and Political Behavior in the United States: The Impact of Beliefs, Affiliations, and Commitment from 1980 to 1994." *Public Opinion Quarterly* 61 (summer): 288–316.

——. 1999. "'Culture Wars' in the American Party System: Religious and Cultural Change among Partisan Activists since 1972." *American Politics Quarterly* 27 (January): 89–121.

———. 2001. *The Great Divide: Religious and Cultural Conflict in American Party Politics.* New York: Columbia University Press.

Layman, Geoffrey C., and Edward G. Carmines. 1997. "Cultural Conflict in American Politics: Religious Traditionalism, Postmaterialism, and U.S. Political Behavior." *Journal of Politics* 59 (August): 751–777.

Layman, Geoffrey C., and Thomas M. Carsey. 2002. "Party Polarization and Party Structuring of Policy Attitudes: A Comparison of Three NES Panel Studies." *Political Behavior* 24 (September): 199–236.

———. 2002. "Party Polarization and 'Conflict Extension' in the American Electorate." *American Journal of Political Science* 46 (October): 786–802.

Lazarsfeld, Paul F., Bernard Berelson, and Hazel Gaudet. 1948. *The People's Choice: How the Voter Makes Up His Mind in a Presidential Campaign,* 2nd edition. New York: Columbia University Press.

Leege, David C., Kenneth D. Wald, Brian S. Krueger, and Paul D. Mueller. 2002. *The Politics of Cultural Differences: Social Change and Voter Mobilization Strategies in the Post-New Deal Period.* Princeton, NJ: Princeton University Press.

Leuchtenburg, William E. 1963. *Franklin D. Roosevelt and the New Deal, 1932–1940.* New York: Harper and Row.

———. 2005. *The White House Looks South: Franklin D. Roosevelt, Harry S. Truman, and Lyndon B. Johnson.* Baton Rouge, LA: Louisiana State University Press.

Levine, Jeffrey, Edward G. Carmines, and Robert Huckfeldt. 1997. "The Rise of Ideology in the Post-New Deal Party System 1972–1992." *American Politics Quarterly* 25 (January): 19–34.

Levinson, Daryl J., and Richard H. Pildes. 2006. "Separation of Parties, Not Powers." *Harvard Law Review* 119 (June): 2312–2386.

Lindaman, Kara, and Donald P. Haider-Markel. 2002. "Issue Evolution, Political Parties, and the Culture Wars." *Political Research Quarterly* 55 (March): 91–110.

Lippmann, Walter. 1922. *Public Opinion.* New York: Harcourt Brace Jovanovich.

Lubell, Samuel. 1956. *The Future of American Politics,* revised edition. Garden City, NY: Doubleday Anchor Books.

MacKuen, Michael B., Robert S. Erikson, James A. Stimson, and Kathleen Knight. 2003. "Elections and the Dynamics of Ideological Representation." In *Electoral Democracy,* edited by Michael B. MacKuen and George Rabinowitz, 200–237. Ann Arbor, MI: University of Michigan Press.

Masuoka, Natalie. 2008. "Defining the Group: Latino Identity and Political Participation." *American Politics Research* 36 (January): 33–61.

Matthews, Donald R., and James W. Prothro. 1964. "Southern Images of Political Parties: An Analysis of White and Negro Attitudes." *Journal of Politics* 26 (February): 82–111.

May, Ann Mari, and Kurt Stephenson. 1994. "Women and the Great Retrenchment: The Political Economy of Gender in the 1980s." *Journal of Economic Issues* 28 (June): 533–542.

Mayer, Jeremy D. 2002. *Running on Race: Racial Politics in Presidential Campaigns, 1960–2000.* New York: Random House.

Mayer, William G. 1992. *The Changing American Mind: How and Why American Public Opinion Changed between 1960 and 1988.* Ann Arbor, MI: University of Michigan Press.

McAdams, John. 2002. "The Dynamics of Voter Attitudes: Reevaluating the Role of Partisanship." Paper presented at the Annual Meeting of the American Political Science Association, Boston, MA.

McConkey, Dale. 2001. "Whither Hunter's Culture War? Shifts in Evangelical Morality, 1988–1998." *Sociology of Religion* 62 (summer): 149–174.

McGerr, Michael E. 1986. *The Decline of Popular Politics: The American North, 1865–1928.* New York: Oxford University Press.

Meier, Kenneth J., Paula D. McClain, J.L. Polinard, and Robert D. Wrinkle. 2004. "Divided or Together? Conflict and Cooperation between African Americans and Latinos." *Political Research Quarterly* 57 (September): 399–409.

Mendelberg, Tali. 2001. *The Race Card: Campaign Strategy, Implicit Messages, and the Norm of Inequality.* Princeton, NJ: Princeton University Press.

Micklethwait, John, and Adrian Wooldridge. 2004. *The Right Nation: Conservative Power in America.* New York: Penguin Press.

Miller, Warren E., and J. Merrill Shanks. 1996. *The New American Voter.* Cambridge, MA: Harvard University Press.

Mueller, Carol M., ed. 1988. *The Politics of the Gender Gap: The Social Construction of Political Influence.* Newbury Park, CA: Sage Publications.

———. 1991. "The Gender Gap and Women's Political Influence." *Annals of the American Academy of Political and Social Science* 515 (May): 23–37.

Myrdal, Gunnar. 1944. *An American Dilemma: The Negro Problem and Modern Democracy.* New York: Harper and Brothers.

Nadeau, Richard, Richard G. Niemi, Harold W. Stanley, and Jean-Francois Godbout. 2004. "Class, Party, and South/Non-South Differences: An Update." *American Politics Research* 32 (January): 52–67.

Nadeau, Richard, and Harold W. Stanley. 1993. "Class Polarization in Partisanship among Native Southern Whites, 1952–1990." *American Journal of Political Science* 37 (August): 900–919.

Nie, Norman H., Sidney Verba, and John R. Petrocik. 1976. *The Changing American Voter.* Cambridge, MA: Harvard University Press.

Norrander, Barbara. 1999. "The Evolution of the Gender Gap." *Public Opinion Quarterly* 63 (winter): 566–576.

Norris, Pippa, and Ronald Inglehart. 2004. *Sacred and Secular: Religion and Politics Worldwide.* New York: Cambridge University Press.

Petrocik, John R. 1996. "Issue Ownership in Presidential Elections, with a 1980 Case Study." *American Journal of Political Science* 40 (August): 825–850.

Petrocik, John R., William L. Benoit, and Glenn J. Hansen. 2003. "Issue Ownership and Presidential Campaigning, 1952–2000." *Political Science Quarterly* 118 (December): 599–626.

Phillips, Kevin P. 1969. *The Emerging Republican Majority.* New Rochelle, NY: Arlington House.

Plotke, David. 1996. *Building a Democratic Political Order: Reshaping American Liberalism in the 1930s and 1940s.* New York: Cambridge University Press.

Pomper, Gerald M. 1971. "Toward a More Responsible Two-party System? What, Again?" *Journal of Politics* 33 (November): 916–940.

———. 1972. "From Confusion to Clarity: Issues and American Voters, 1956–1968." *American Political Science Review* 66 (June): 415–428.

———. 1975. *Voters' Choice: Varieties of American Electoral Behavior.* New York: Dodd, Mead, and Company.

——— . 2001. "The 2000 Presidential Election: Why Gore Lost." *Political Science Quarterly* 116 (summer): 201–223.

Pomper, Gerald M., and Marc D. Weiner. 2002. "Toward a More Responsible Two-party Voter: The Evolving Bases of Partisanship." In *Responsible Partisanship? The Evolution of American Parties Since 1950*, edited by John C. Green and Paul S. Herrnson, 181–200. Lawrence, KS: University Press of Kansas.

Poole, Keith T., and Howard Rosenthal. 1984. "The Polarization of American Politics." *Journal of Politics* 46 (November): 1061–1079.

——— . 1991. "Patterns of Congressional Voting." *American Journal of Political Science* 35 (February): 228–278.

——— . 1997. *Congress: A Political–Economic History of Roll Call Voting.* New York: Oxford University Press.

Popkin, Samuel L. 1991. *The Reasoning Voter: Communication and Persuasion in Presidential Campaigns.* Chicago: University of Chicago Press.

Rae, Nicol C. 1989. *The Decline and Fall of the Liberal Republicans from 1952 to the Present.* New York: Oxford University Press.

——— . 1992. "Class and Culture: American Political Cleavages in the Twentieth Century." *Western Political Quarterly* 45 (September): 629–650.

Rahn, Wendy M. 1993. "The Role of Partisan Stereotypes in Information Processing about Political Candidates." *American Journal of Political Science* 37 (May): 472–496.

RePass, David E. 1971. "Issue Salience and Party Choice." *American Political Science Review* 65 (June): 389–400.

Rohde, David W. 1991. *Parties and Leaders in the Postreform House.* Chicago: University of Chicago Press.

Sanbonmatsu, Kira. 2002. *Democrats, Republicans, and the Politics of Women's Place.* Ann Arbor, MI: University of Michigan Press.

Sanchez, Gabriel R. 2008. "Latino Group Consciousness and Perceptions of Commonality with African Americans." *Social Science Quarterly* 89 (June): 428–444.

Sanders, Arthur. 1988. "The Meaning of Party Images." *Western Political Quarterly* 41 (September): 583–599.

Saunders, Kyle L., and Alan I. Abramowitz. 2004. "Ideological Realignment and Active Partisans in the American Electorate." *American Politics Research* 32 (May): 285–309.

Scammon, Richard M., and Ben J. Wattenberg. 1970. *The Real Majority.* New York: Coward-McCann.

Schattschneider, E.E. 1942. *Party Government.* New York: Holt, Rinehart, and Winston.

Schlesinger, Arthur, Jr. 1960. *The Politics of Upheaval.* Boston: Houghton Mifflin.

Schlesinger, Mark, and Caroline Heldman. 2001. "Gender Gap or Gender Gaps? New Perspectives on Support for Government Action and Policies." *Journal of Politics* 63 (February): 59–92.

Schreckhise, William D., and Todd G. Shields. 2003. "Ideological Realignment in the Contemporary U.S. Electorate Revisited." *Social Science Quarterly* 84 (September): 596–612.

Schuman, Howard, Charlotte Steeh, Lawrence Bobo, and Maria Krysan. 1997. *Racial Attitudes in America: Trends and Interpretations*, revised edition. Cambridge, MA: Harvard University Press.

Sears, David O. 1988. "Symbolic Racism." In *Eliminating Racism: Profiles in Controversy*, edited by Phyllis A. Katz and Dalmas A. Taylor, 53–84. New York: Plenum Press.

Sears, David O., and P.J. Henry. 2003. "The Origins of Symbolic Racism." *Journal of Personality and Social Psychology* 85: (August): 259–275.

Sears, David O., P.J. Henry, and Rick Kosterman. 2000. "Egalitarian Values and Contemporary Racial Politics." In *Racialized Politics: The Debate about Racism in America*, edited by David O. Sears, Jim Sidanius, and Lawrence Bobo, 75–117. Chicago: University of Chicago Press.

Sears, David O., John J. Hetts, Jim Sidanius, and Lawrence Bobo, "Race in American Politics: Framing the Debate." In *Racialized Politics: The Debate about Racism in America*, edited by David O. Sears, Jim Sidanius, and Lawrence Bobo, 1–43. Chicago: University of Chicago Press.

Sears, David O., and Donald R. Kinder. 1971. "Racial Tension and Voting in Los Angeles." In *Los Angeles: Viability and Prospects for Metropolitan Leadership*, edited by Werner Z. Hirsch, 51–88. New York: Praeger.

Sellers, Charles. 1965. "The Equilibrium Cycle in Two-party Politics." *Public Opinion Quarterly* 29 (spring): 16–38.

Seltzer, Richard A., Jody Newman, and Melissa Voorhees Leighton. 1997. *Sex as a Political Variable: Women as Candidates and Voters in U.S. Elections*. Boulder, CO: Lynne Rienner.

Shafer, Byron E. 1985. "The New Cultural Politics." *PS* 18 (spring): 221–231.

Shafer, Byron E., and Richard Johnston. 2006. *The End of Southern Exceptionalism: Class, Race, and Partisan Change in the Postwar South*. Cambridge, MA: Harvard University Press.

Shapiro, Robert Y., and Harpeet Mahajan. 1986. "Gender Differences in Policy Preferences: A Summary of Trends from the 1960s to the 1980s." *Public Opinion Quarterly* 50 (spring): 42–61.

Sidanius, Jim, Pam Singh, John J. Hetts, and Chris Federico. 2000. "It's Not Affirmative Action, It's the Blacks: The Continuing Relevance of Race in American Politics." In *Racialized Politics: The Debate about Racism in America*, edited by David O. Sears, Jim Sidanius, and Lawrence Bobo, 191–235. Chicago: University of Chicago Press.

Sigelman, Lee, and Susan Welch. 1991. *Black Americans' Views of Racial Inequality: The Dream Deferred*. New York: Cambridge University Press.

Sinclair, Barbara. 2002. "The Dream Fulfilled? Party Development in Congress, 1950–2000." In *Responsible Partisanship? The Evolution of American Parties Since 1950*, edited by John C. Green and Paul S. Herrnson, 121–140. Lawrence, KS: University Press of Kansas.

——— . 2006. *Party Wars: Polarization and the Politics of National Policy Making*. Norman, OK: University of Oklahoma Press.

Smith, Tom W. 1984. "The Polls: Gender and Attitudes toward Violence." *Public Opinion Quarterly* 48 (spring): 384–396.

Sniderman, Paul M., Richard A. Brody, and Philip E. Tetlock. 1991. *Reasoning and Choice: Explorations in Political Psychology*. New York: Cambridge University Press.

Sniderman, Paul M., and Edward G. Carmines. 1997. *Reaching Beyond Race*. Cambridge, MA: Harvard University Press.

Sniderman, Paul M., Gretchen Crosby, and William G. Howell. 2000. "The Politics of Race." In *Racialized Politics: The Debate about Racism in America*, edited
by David O. Sears, Jim Sidanius, and Lawrence Bobo, 236–279. Chicago: University of Chicago Press.

Sniderman, Paul M., and Thomas Piazza. 1993. *The Scar of Race*. Cambridge, MA:
Belknap Press of Harvard University Press.

Stanga, John E., and James F. Sheffield. 1987. "The Myth of Zero Partisanship:
Attitudes toward American Political Parties, 1964–1984." *American Journal of
Political Science* 31 (November): 829–855.

Stanley, Harold W., and Richard G. Niemi. 1991. "Partisanship and Group Support, 1952–1988." *American Politics Quarterly* 19 (April): 189–210.

——— . 2001. "Party Coalitions in Transition: Partisanship and Group Support,
1952–1996." In *Controversies in Voting Behavior*, 4th edition, edited by Richard
G. Niemi and Herbert F. Weisberg, 387–404. Washington, DC: CQ Press.

Steeh, Charlotte. 1995. Review of *The Scar of Race*, by Paul M. Sniderman and
Thomas Piazza. *Public Opinion Quarterly* 59 (summer): 316–319.

Stimson, James A. 2004. *Tides of Consent: How Public Opinion Shapes American
Politics*. New York: Cambridge University Press.

Stonecash, Jeffrey M. 2000. *Class and Party in American Politics*. Boulder, CO:
Westview Press.

——— . 2006. *Political Parties Matter: Realignment and the Return of Partisan Voting*.
Boulder, CO: Lynne Rienner.

Stonecash, Jeffrey M., Mark D. Brewer, and Mack D. Mariani. 2003. *Diverging
Parties: Social Change, Realignment, and Party Polarization*. Boulder, CO:
Westview Press.

Stonecash, Jeffrey M., Mark D. Brewer, Mary P. McGuire, R. Eric Petersen, and
Lori Beth Way. 2000. "Class and Party: Secular Realignment and the Survival
of Democrats Outside of the South." *Political Research Quarterly* 53 (December):
731–752.

Stroh, Patrick K. 1995. "Voters as Pragmatic Cognitive Misers: The Accuracy–
Effort Trade-off in the Candidate Evaluation Process." In *Political Judgment:
Structure and Process*, edited by Milton Lodge and Kathleen M. McGraw,
207–228. Ann Arbor, MI: University of Michigan Press.

Tarman, Christopher, and David O. Sears. 2005. "The Conceptualization and
Measurement of Symbolic Racism." *Journal of Politics* 67 (August): 731–761.

Tate, Katherine. 1993. *From Protest to Politics: The New Black Voters in American
Elections*. New York and Cambridge, MA: Russell Sage Foundation and
Harvard University Press.

Taylor, Andrew J. 1996. "The Ideological Development of the Parties in Washington, 1947–1994." *Polity* 29 (winter): 273–292.

Taylor, Shelley E., and Susan T. Fiske. 1978. "Salience, Attention, and Attribution:
Top of the Head Phenomena." In *Advances in Experimental Social Psychology*,
edited by Leonard Berkowitz, 250–258. New York: Academic Press.

Tocqueville, Alexis de. 1990. *Democracy in America*, 2 vols, edited by Phillips
Bradley. New York: Vintage Books.

Trilling, Richard J. 1976. *Party Image and Electoral Behavior*. New York: John Wiley
& Sons.

Tuch, Steven A., Lee Sigelman, and Jack K. Martin. 1997. "Fifty Years after

Myrdal: Blacks' Policy Attitudes in the 1990s." In *Racial Attitudes in the 1990s: Continuity and Change*, edited by Steven A. Tuch and Jack K. Martin. Westport, CT: Praeger.

Wald, Kenneth D., and Corwin E. Smidt. 1993. "Measurement Strategies in the Study of Religion and Politics." In *Rediscovering the Religious Factor in American Politics*, edited by David C. Leege and Lyman A. Kellstedt, 26–49. Armonk, NY: M.E. Sharpe.

Wattenberg, Martin P. 1987. "The Hollow Realignment: Partisan Change in a Candidate-centered Era." *Public Opinion Quarterly* 51 (spring): 58–74.

———. 1991. "The Building of a Republican Regional Base in the South: The Elephant Crosses the Mason–Dixon Line." *Public Opinion Quarterly* 55 (autumn): 424–431.

———. 1998. *The Decline of American Political Parties, 1952–1996*. Cambridge, MA: Harvard University Press.

Way, H. Frank, Jr. 1968. "Survey Research on Judicial Decisions: The Prayer and Bible Reading Cases." *Western Political Quarterly* 21 (June): 189–205.

White, John Kenneth. 2003. *The Values Divide: American Politics and Culture in Transition*. New York: Chatham House Publishers.

Wiebe, Robert H. 1967. *The Search for Order, 1877–1920*. New York: Hill and Wang.

Wildavsky, Aaron. 1965. "The Goldwater Phenomenon: Purists, Politicians, and the Two-party System." *Review of Politics* 27 (July): 386–413.

Williams, Rhys, ed. 1997. *Cultural Wars in American Politics: Critical Reviews of a Popular Myth*. New York: Aldine de Gruyter.

Wilson, William Julius. 1996. *When Work Disappears: The World of the New Urban Poor*. New York: Random House.

Wirls, Daniel. 1986. "Reinterpreting the Gender Gap." *Public Opinion Quarterly* 50 (autumn): 316–330.

Wolbrecht, Christina. 2000. *The Politics of Women's Rights: Parties, Positions, and Change*. Princeton, NJ: Princeton University Press.

Wuthnow, Robert. 1988. *The Restructuring of American Religion: Society and Faith Since World War II*. Princeton, NJ: Princeton University Press.

———. 1989. *The Struggle for America's Soul: Evangelicals, Liberals, and Secularism*. Grand Rapids, MI: William B. Eerdmans Publishing Company.

Zaller, John R. 1992. *The Nature and Origins of Mass Opinion*. New York: Cambridge University Press.

Index

Ickes, Harold 36
ideology: polarization 3
income distribution: economic images 26;
   family income 23; non-economic
   domestic images 26; party images
   23–31; party philosophy images 29;
   presidential vote 23; see also class
Inglehart, Ronald 21

Jackman, Mary 35
Jarvis, Sharon 4

Kaufmann, Karen 49
Kenski, Henry 49
Key, V.O. 2, 20
Kinder, Donald 34
King, Martin Luther 33

Latinos 35, 37
Lazarsfeld, Paul 2
Levinson, Daryl 3
Lippmann, Walter xii

Mayer, William 22
men: gender gap see gender
Myrdal, Gunnar 33

NAACP 36
New Deal 17, 20, 21, 22, 35–6, 61, 74
Nie, Norman 2
non-economic domestic images: changes
   14; Democratic Party 14, 40, 69; gender
   57; income distribution 26; meaning 12;
   race/ethnicity 40; religion 69;
   Republican Party 14, 57; significance 75

partisan evaluation: political process xii
partisanship: citizenship 3–4; conflict 4;
   elites 3
party images: categories 12–17; class
   20–32; class divisions 23–32; economic
   see economic images; electorate as a
   whole 7–19; foreign policy see foreign
   policy images; gender 48–60; general see
   general party images; government see
   non-economic domestic images; income
   levels 23–31; likes/dislikes 5, 7–12,
   17–18, 23–32, 37–46, 52–60, 65–73;
   mass political alignment 2; no mentions
   12; non-economic see non-economic
   domestic images; party affect 11, 26, 40,
   54; people see people in the party

images; philosophy see party
   philosophy images; pictures of parties
   1–6; prevalence 8–11; race/ethnicity
   33–47; racial/ethnic divide 37–46;
   religion 61–73; salience 9, 10, 23–4, 38,
   52, 61–73; sex 51–60; significance 1–4,
   77–9
party philosophy images: decrease 14;
   Democratic Party 14, 19, 40, 57; gender
   57; income distribution 29; meaning 12;
   race/ethnicity 40, 47; Republican Party
   14, 17, 19, 29, 57, 75
people in the party images: candidate-
   centered politics 14; Democratic Party
   14; meaning 12; Republican Party 17
Phillips, Kevin 21
philosophy see party philosophy images
Piazza, Thomas 34
Pildes, Richard 3
Popkin, Samuel 5
Populists 20
presidential vote: church attendance 64;
   gender 49; income distribution 23; race/
   ethnicity 37
Progressive Era 20

race/ethnicity: Democratic Party 37–8, 39,
   41–2, 46–7; economic images 40, 47;
   general party images 30, 42; inequality
   33, 35; non-economic domestic images
   40; party images 33–47; party
   philosophy images 40, 47; presidential
   vote 37; racial/ethnic divide 37–46;
   Republican Party 38–42, 44–6;
   significance 34–7; symbolic/new racism
   34
Rae, Nicol 21
Reagan, Ronald Wilson (40th President)
   22, 36–7, 64
religion: cultural issues 62, 63, 64;
   Democratic Party 65–70; liberalism/
   conservatism 62; non-economic
   domestic images 69; party images
   61–73; religious salience 61–73;
   Republican Party 66–7, 69, 71–3; right/
   wrong 63; Supreme Court decisions 62
Republican Party: big business 17, 20, 29;
   conservatism 8, 17, 36; economic
   images 14; foreign policy images 17, 29;
   gender 49–50, 53–4, 57–60; general
   party images 17; government
   management images 14; individualism

Controversies in Electoral Democracy and Representation

Edited by **Matthew Streb**, Northern Illinois University

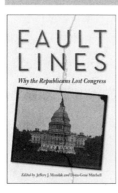

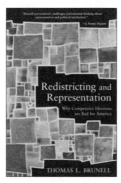

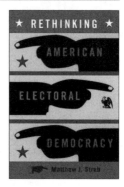

Fault Lines: Why the Republicans Lost Congress
Edited by Jeffery Mondak and Dona-Gene Mitchell

"Fault Lines offers a multitude of insights into the historic mid-term elections of 2006. The chapters are accessible and engaging, and the opening remarks from Lee Hamilton, a senior statesman in American politics, underscore the significance of this work."
—James A. McCann, Purdue University

August 2008: 192pp
Hb: 978-0-415-99361-6
Pb: 978-0-415-99362-3

Redistricting and Representation: Why Competitive Elections are Bad for America
Thomas Brunell

"Professor Brunell provocatively challenges conventional thinking... He convincingly argues that electoral competition is not, nor perhaps should it be, the hallmark of democracy."
—J. Dennis Hastert (IL-14), Speaker of the United States House of Representatives (1999-2007)

February 2008: 160pp
Hb: 978-0-415-96452-4
Pb: 978-0-415-96453-1

Rethinking American Electoral Democracy
Matthew Streb

"Do we vote too often, and for too many offices? Neither conservative nor liberal, populist nor elitist, *Rethinking American Electoral Democracy* is a major contribution to efforts to improve and perfect our democratic institutions."
—Bradley Smith, Capitol University Law School, and former Chair of the Federal Election Commission

June 2008: 240pp
Hb: 978-0-415-96138-7
Pb: 978-0-415-96139-4